From Abused to Protector:

"Claiming Your Life After Your Church Sexually Abuses You"

A Story of Hope, Forgiveness and Triumph

By
Kenneth F. Joe Sr.

© Copyright 2007, Kenneth F. Joe Sr.

All Rights Reserved.

No part of this book may be reproduced, stored in a retrieval system, or transmitted by any means, electronic, mechanical, photocopying, recording, or otherwise, without written permission from the author.

ISBN: 978-0-6151-6047-4

To purchase additional copies or to contact the author, please visit: **www.CareEnough.net**

Or Mail a Check for $19.99 (Shipping Included) to:
Care Enough
P.O. Box 43723
Atlanta, GA 30336

Table of Contents

About the Author: .... Pages: iv-viii

Acknowledgments: .... Page: viii

Foreword: .... Page: ix

Scene 1 – The Inquest: .... Pages: 1-41

**Scene 2 – Where I have been, Where I am and Where
we must go:** .... Pages: 42-54

Scene 3 – Life After the Abuse: .... Pages: 55-65

Scene 4 – Thoughts and Reflections: .... Pages: 66-78

Scene 5 – Closure: .... Pages: 79-89

"IF WE <u>CARE ENOUGH</u> WE CAN MAKE A DIFFERENCE"

Professional Biography
Kenneth F. Joe, Sr., MS, MS
www.careenough.net

Having been sexually abused by the pastor of his Church for six years, Kenneth F. Joe Sr., considers himself a survivor and not a victim. After settling one of the largest cases in the history of the Archdiocese of Chicago in June of 2006, Kenneth tells his story now as inspiration and hope to those who have found themselves betrayed by their Church and struggle to move forward.

Kenneth F. Joe Sr., is the Current Director of Integrated Family Support for the Georgia Department of Human Resources, the Former Director of Fulton (Atlanta) County Department of Family & Children Services (DFCS), the largest public Child Welfare System in Georgia and the former DFCS Director of Richmond County (Augusta, second largest city in Georgia). He was the Interim Executive Director and the Chief Operating Officer of Chicago Child Care Society, the oldest Child Welfare agency in the state of Illinois. He has worked in Child Welfare for 17 years.

Born and raised in Chicago, Illinois, Kenneth F. Joe, Sr. credits his success in life to a family foundation rooted in Christian values. The second youngest of eight children, Kenneth learned that life is much easier when you share and listen to the wisdom of those who came before you. Although he spent many of his formative years growing up in the Wentworth Garden Housing Projects in Chicago, Kenneth reflects "Even though we were poor, we didn't feel it because we had love and discipline in our home." From his humble beginnings, Kenneth went on to earn a Bachelor of Arts degree in Political Science with a minor in Social Work from Lewis University in Romeoville, Illinois, a Masters of Science degree in Human Services Administration from Spertus College in Chicago, Illinois, and a Masters of Science degree in Clinical Counseling from National-Lewis University in Chicago, Illinois.

Mr. Joe's philosophy is that the only limitations in life are those, which we place upon ourselves: "Challenges make us stronger and can be used as motivation to succeed and overcome. Never allow outside limitations to determine your success in life. The expectations you set in your mind and in your heart should be the driving force that pushes you to achieve your dreams." Determined to apply this philosophy, Kenneth used his sexual abuse as a driving force to begin his career in the late 80's counseling male youth at Joliet Job Corps Center in Joliet, Illinois. He provided ongoing supervision to 30 males ranging in ages from 12 – 21 years of age and evaluated each youth's progress to ensure personal growth and life skills. From there Kenneth went on to become a youth advocate at Guardian Angel Home in Joliet, Illinois providing counseling and crisis intervention to at-risk youth. Performing all the duties of a case manager from engaging local law enforcement to completing home assessments, Kenneth gained front-line experience dealing with the challenges of Child Welfare.

Kenneth continued to strive to help those most vulnerable to the stresses of life, particularly children and the elderly. Over an eight-year period Kenneth worked in several supervisory capacities at various youth programs in Chicago, Illinois aimed at improving academic achievement, reducing adolescent pregnancy and increasing employment opportunities for youth.

In the late 90's Kenneth continued to actively engage in efforts to improve community and public systems servicing children, youth and families. As Associate Director of Youth Welfare Services at Chicago Youth Centers, Kenneth was in charge of a $3,000,000 budget and assumed full responsibility of running the day-to-day operations of a Child Welfare Program.

From there he went on to become the Director of Residential Services at St. Joseph's Carondelet Child Center, a treatment center for hard to place at-risk adolescents. Supervising an Independent Living Program and facilitating an expansion project, which increased the center's population capacity, Kenneth's commitment to the well-being of adolescents never wavered. As Senior Vice President of Treatment for Mercy Home for Boys and Girls, Kenneth was responsible for developing policies and insuring compliance with state standards. Working with a team of other professionals, Kenneth helped to facilitate one of the biggest expansions in the history of the organization. In addition, Kenneth supervised 5 Master Level Program Directors as well as the day-to-day operations of the treatment facility. During his tenure at Mercy Home for Boys and Girls, Kenneth performed some of the most rewarding work in his career and benefited professionally as a person from the team philosophy of the organization.

Serving in two capacities at the Chicago Child Care Society, Kenneth displayed his multifaceted social services skills by serving as the Chief of Operations as well as the Interim Executive Director. As Chief of Operations he would oversee the day-to-day operations of the agency assuming responsibility of a $4,000,000 budget, recruitment of staff and board members as well as the development of new programs to solicit revenue for the agency. Transitioning into the Interim Executive Director position, he was able to further the agency's efforts by securing new contracts in excess of $600,000 which included collaboration with Chicago Public Schools to work in 17 Chicago

High Schools in order to provide services to pregnant and parenting students.

Advancing his vision for youth and families, Kenneth began work as the Director of Richmond County Department of Family and Children Services (DFCS), a Class V Child Welfare Office located in Augusta, Georgia. Supervising a staff of over 200 and responsible for an operation budget of over $13 million, Kenneth streamlined agency hiring processes, eliminated caseworker vacancies, reduced caseloads, and instituted numerous other agency modifications to improve the quality of service for its clients. Under his leadership, Kenneth decreased Temporary Assistance for Needy Families (TANF) recipients by nearly 60% and increased work participation rates from 54% to 75% in one year.

Due to his success in Richmond, Kenneth was appointed the Administrator of Fulton County DFCS the largest public Child Welfare System in the state of Georgia. In this role he over-saw the direct services and program areas including Office of Family Independence, Social Services Section, Financial Services, Human Resources and Program Support. His supervision included the development, monitoring, and maintenance of, $110 million budget, a staff of over 1100 and the establishment and maintenance of partnerships with various public and private groups.

Kenneth has been married to his wife Lisa for 10 years and they are blessed with one son, Kenneth F. Joe Jr. He is a member of NAACP/Silver Life – Fayette County Ga., Rainbow Push Coalition, Omega Psi Phi Fraternity, Inc./Life Member # 3628 and the Lewis University Alumni Association.

Acknowledgments

A special thanks to my wife Lisa who is my daily support and quiet strength. Your love has helped give me the courage to share this very private and difficult story. To my son Kenneth Jr. for being born and who along with all children inspire me to do all I can to ensure that the Roman Catholic Church and society never again give sanctuary to pedophiles. Lastly, to my mentors in Child Welfare; Dr. Blasingame, Donald Dew and Denice Murray thank you for your guidance in molding me as a person and a Child Welfare Professional. Your dedication to children make you my heroes.

David my brother, always know that I love you.

Foreword

In writing this book I have chosen to tell my story in language that is as hurtful as the sexual abuse the children of the Roman Catholic Church have had to endure. For those who share my pain, I hope to tell a story that you can be proud of. You can overcome your hurt by reclaiming your life. Give no more silence to the betrayal of your Church.

I live with my scars everyday. However, I choose to forgive my abuser for his predatory actions against me. My Church for its "don't know, don't tell attitude". And my Parish/Church Community of adults for seeing the signs daily and being blinded by the perceived innocence of the Church/Clergy.

I pledge my life to the protection of children now. I pledge to be a champion for the innocent always………no matter where it takes me.

"IF WE CARE ENOUGH WE CAN MAKE A DIFFERENCE"

Mother to Son
by
Langston Hughes

Well, son, I'll tell you:
Life for me ain't been no **crystal stair.**
It's had **tacks in it**,
And **splinters**,
And **boards torn up**,
And places with no carpet on the floor—
Bare.
But all the time
I'se been a-climbin' on,
And **reachin' landin's**,
And turnin' corners,
And sometimes **goin' in the dark**
Where there **ain't been no light.**
So boy, **don't you turn back.**
Don't you set down on the steps
'Cause you finds it's **kinder hard.**
Don't you fall now—
For I'se still goin', honey,
I'se still climbin',
And life for me ain't been no crystal stair.

"IF WE CARE ENOUGH WE CAN MAKE A DIFFERENCE"

Scene 1

As for me, I will call upon God, and the Lord shall save me. Evening and morning and at noon I will pray, and cry aloud, And He shall hear my voice. He has redeemed my soul in peace from the battle that was against me.

PSALM 55:16-18

The Inquest

It had taken me a long time to decide whether or not to bring the story of my abuse to the authorities. Unfortunately, now that I had made the decision to do so, my abuser, Fr. Victor Edward Stewart (Fr. V.), was deceased and some might feel what is the point in telling the story now. I tell my story now for me and those who have also lived through sexual abuse at the sacrifice of their Church failing them.

The inquest was held on December 5, 2005 at 3:00p.m. at the Chicago office of the Archdiocese of Chicago. Present were myself, Attorney Phillip Aaron and his paralegal Mr. Richie Aaron. Also present were Dr. Bland, Assistance Ministry of the Archdiocese and Ms. Patricia Zacharias of the Office of Professional Responsibility. Ms. Zacharias explained as I talked that her role was to take notes and to prepare the draft of the report afterwards. She then gave me an envelope with information pertaining to the Illinois Department of Children and Family Services and the State's Attorney's Office. I was also provided with a copy of the Archdiocese of Chicago policy: *1100 Sexual Abuse of Minors: Policies for Education, Prevention, Assistance to Victims and Procedures for Determination of Fitness for Ministry. I remember sitting there listening to the tone of Dr. Bland wondering why would he be in this capacity? His tone and approach was cold and uncaring. I had to remind myself that I was not here for him. Don't get caught up in his personality. Tell your story and get out of here.*

Attorney Aaron told me that he was familiar with the information Ms. Zacharias provided to me and he could review it with me if I wished. After working in Foster Care/Child Welfare for the past 15 years, I would be considered by some standards "very qualified" in this area so I declined any further assistance in the review of the material.

Ms. Zacharias asked me to begin wherever I felt most comfortable. She advised she might have some questions herself, at the end.

I thought I would be hesitant and nervous. It had been such a long time and now it would all be out in the open. But I wasn't hesitant. In fact, I was eager. Finally, I would get it out. I had learned that confession was good for the soul and I needed this cleansing more than I needed anything before in my life.

As I looked at the faces around the table, I cleared my throat and said, "I've been working in Child Welfare for sixteen years and I've never had to give the detail I am about to give. I have never even spoken to my wife in this kind of detail. I've tried to put this behind me for many years. The times I did find the courage to try to deal with it I did not receive any assistance, so I had to *not* deal with it. When I approached Father P and told him about it, his advice to me was to pray about it. About the time Fr. V. got sick, I called Bishop Goedert, the Vicar for Priests at the time and I talked to him on the phone, outlining the abuse. I was met mostly with dead silence and by the end of the phone call complete silence." So this was my first encounter with Church authorities and it wasn't hard to see their position. There would be no support. The Church cover-up was in high gear.

At that point I was admonished for editorializing and asked to just give the facts and leave the decision making to others. I reminded Dr. Bland that this was my story and I will tell it to my satisfaction. Feeling that twisting of my words would be the final outcome, I wanted to make sure that my story was told in my words, with my emotion and ultimately through my pain. I remember feeling angry at the defensiveness that I perceived coming from Dr. Bland. He made me feel he did not want to hear the pain. He seemed to want to get through it and send me on my way. I told myself, "continue don't let him take you away from what you came to say". I continued with my story.

"I met Fr. V. before he was officially installed at our parish. He had begun living in the rectory and was already active in the Parish before his official installation ceremony. This was sometime in 1982. I was in the seventh grade and aware that Fr. V. was coming to St. Charles Lwanga. I was a good Catholic boy and involved in every aspect of parish life, from altar boy to volunteer in almost anything church related. I was really excited that Father was coming to the parish and I was happy that he was black. I had been baptized, had my first communion and went to school in the Parish. My whole life was built around home and St. Charles Lwanga. A black pastor was a first and it was the first time I was to see a black man up-close in a position of authority.

"I remember the first time I met Fr. V. In fact I'll never forget it. I was standing on the school steps. He wasn't wearing his collar, so I didn't recognize him as a priest. He asked me, 'Who are you?'

"I said, 'I'm Kenneth Frederick Nolan and who are you?'

"He told me he was Fr. Victor Edward Stewart the new pastor, and I remember feeling embarrassed that I had just come across as a smart-aleck to the new pastor! It meant nothing then, but now I know the kind smile that he gave me was really filled with lust. I believe at that moment I became prey for Fr. V.

"Soon I was being encouraged by Fr. V. to hang out with him. A troubled, poor kid I had never done any 'hanging out.' He had some of his godsons from his previous parishes visiting him at the rectory of St. Charles Lwanga. They all followed him around like he was a god. I remember feeling that I wanted to be liked by Fr. V. too! I want to be special and go to restaurants, bowling and movies! In fact, I did feel special when he "chose me" to hang out with them.

"I began to spend time with these older boys. We went bowling, to the movies, etc. I was the youngest of the group, about twelve at the time. The other boys were about 18-early twenties. They had followed Fr. V. from his previous parishes and seemed to love him very much. He had a connection with them. It was like everyday was

Christmas! I lived in the projects and was dirt poor. Our refrigerator was often empty and I was often a little bit more hungry after each meal. So something like bowling and after bowling snacks, which were sumptuous, like banana splits and Sundays and sodas was a real treat. My siblings were jealous of me and there was some resentment, but I was a kid and again this was irresistible for me.

"At Christmas time Fr. V. began buying me gifts. He bought me video games like Frogger and Donkey Kong and a portable television set. These were unheard of luxuries and I can tell you my brothers and sisters were very confused about where all this stuff was coming from. They didn't understand what was happening. I thought everything was great and my mother never questioned the gifts or to my knowledge asked him to stop buying them.

"Around July of 1982, sometime during the summer, Fr. V. began taking me to Ford City shopping Center to buy clothes. I had never been to such a place. I can only remember going to Evergreen Plaza once or twice. Fr. V. took me to the GAP and bought me corduroy pants in every color. I had never gone shopping and felt I could have what ever I wanted in the store. I was astonished. I had no constant father figure, no male, in my life and I craved one. My biological father came around every so often. I wished he would have been around more. Fr. V. was heaven sent for me. I had never seen the play *Pygmalion*, but if I had, Fr. V. was my Henry Higgins. He was opening up a whole new world for me, a world that as it happened made me the envy of many. Little did I know that there was a price to be paid for that status.

"I remember school beginning when the first incident happened. It was the day after we had gone shopping. Fr. V. and I were watching TV on the second floor in the rectory. The TV room had three black leather couches, and a large screen TV, utter luxury for a ghetto kid. I had been in this parish for as long as I could remember. I had been baptized and made my first Communion there. I had been in that school since 1st grade and never had I been in the upstairs rooms of the rectory until Fr. V. arrived. I truly felt special and in the "in crowd."

"It started out with a hug. There was nothing unusual about this as he always hugged me. I was always around, spending many a night at the rectory when we had gone to a movie. He'd call my mother and tell her I was spending the night. So it wasn't anything unusual. Well, one of these sleep over nights he was hugging me close and then he began to unbutton my shirt. Without saying anything he began rubbing my nipples. Soon, it was more than my nipples that was erect. I felt odd, strange. I wasn't sure this was supposed to happen. In fact, I was embarrassed. I remember I felt like screaming and running out the door. Just then Father K, the Associate Pastor and a long time friend of Fr. V. walked into the room and I thought it was over, and at least I wouldn't have to struggle with my feelings. The two of them had a brief conversation, and Fr. V. never moved his hand from down my shirt. Fr. K just stood there and did nothing as Fr. V. sat hugging me with his one arm that he had down my shirt. Fr. V. got up and locked the door after Fr. K walked out. *I knew from this day that Fr. K would not be the adult savior that would stop the abuse.*

"I knew something was happening when he took me to his bedroom and took my clothes off. He looked at my body like it was something special, a work of art. I remember him looking at me like he wanted to consume me! He then got undressed and carried me to the bed. He lay down next to me and began to kiss me. I got uncomfortable when he tried to push his tongue into my mouth. I was rather shocked and it seemed so surreal I wasn't sure it was happening. The sensations were so strange and other worldly. Then he stroked my penis. He began to suck my nipples. I ejaculated for the first time, a very strange, but pleasurable sensation. He then showed me how to perform oral sex and guided me into a position where we could perform on each other.

"I later remember anger. I had never dreamed that this was the way I would lose my virginity. Like most boys I had dreamed of girls, my ideal girl and how it would be to be in love. To make love. Yes, I was mad. He had robbed me of that special initiation into the world of sex and love." I remember lying in the bed that night wondering if I was now gay. What would my friends say! Would they be able to tell that something happened! The morning came and I had no time to run because we went out to breakfast and then shopping. This would be the pattern of his manipulation of my mind.

I looked around the room trying to gauge their reactions as I spilled out all of the sordid details. I had always thought that I would feel embarrassed and uncomfortable, yet that wasn't really the case. Instead, there was a feeling of relief as I unleashed the truth one word at a time. I continued with my story.

"Now, about this time, I was having trouble in school, or rather I was always in trouble at school. With my mother's responsibilities she had little time to try to straighten me out. She had no time for a problem child. Besides, I wasn't her favorite. So it was decided by Fr. V. and my mother that I would move into the rectory. The idea was that this would be a kind of 'boot camp' and it would straighten me out. Of course, Fr. V. had other ideas about me and my future. I remember being mad at my mother for allowing this to happen. I felt like she had given me to him for him to do with me as he pleased. She seemed to love him. She did not know that this action made me feel like she hated me.

"My room was on the second floor which is the same floor Father K's was on. Ms. B, another priest's mother, was the housekeeper. I always felt that she didn't like me. She certainly wasn't nice to me. However, it wasn't personal with Ms. B, she didn't seem to like any of the kids. Before Fr. V. came to the parish Ms. B ruled that rectory with a stern voice and a fast but wobbly walk. She didn't allow children past the kitchen and when you had to go beyond those confines she watched you like a hawk. I know Ms. B felt like all the rules had changed because there were now kids able to roam the rectory freely. I know now that by Fr. V. making this the norm, adults would not ask questions as to why the children were upstairs with him. During these years as we have gathered from other abuse stories, one wouldn't dare think or question the actions of a priest.

"By now Fr. V. and I were a 'couple.' We went everywhere together and the sexual abuse had progressed to anal sex. One night when I slept with Father he told me I was his 'wife.' I remember that term kind of conflicting with my self-image as an adolescent boy, but one didn't argue with Father. As I said, what he wanted he got. One night while we were in bed together, naked, he made us take 'vows.' This made me feel as odd as the 'you're my wife' comment. But rather than rock the boat I told him all this was fine with me. He told me he was going to buy us rings. He took me to a religious store on the north side of Chicago and bought us both sterling silver crucifixion rings. He told me to where it at all times. I still have the ring.

"About this time I graduated from grammar school but I was having more problems than ever. My official reports list all kinds of behavior problems. I know that my abuse was exasperating these problems. It got so bad that there was a two-month period where I didn't go to school at all. The school would send homework and I would do it in bed at the rectory. This was the 8th grade.

"Our relationship was sometimes rocky. When I didn't perform the way he wanted sexually he would get mad and be mean to me. He'd make me sit on the floor to do my homework. There were days when he demanded, 'Don't get dressed.' He would then lock the door with a deadbolt. I had the key to the bedroom and access to the bathroom. He would lock the door not to keep me in, but to keep people out. I wouldn't consider opening the door, out of fear of getting in trouble. The housekeeper didn't have a key. It was like living as husband and wife and I was the less than enthusiastic wife who had to suffer the husband's wrath.

"Fr. V. enrolled me in Quigley South Seminary acting as my guardian. He was listed as the main contact person. My mother was not listed anywhere. This made me feel as though my mother had thrown me away.

"I was uncomfortable at Quigley, especially hating showering with other boys. I don't know the reason for this. Nobody else seemed to mind. I had to guess it had something to do with my special situation. I also felt uncomfortable meeting with priests other than Fr. V. I guess I was paranoid, thinking they all knew about me. And they would want their share of me. My time at Quigley was full of academic struggles and disciplinary issues. Eventually, fights and disruptive behavior would have me transfer to Willibrord Catholic High School. The school was co-ed so I was much more comfortable in this setting. Fr. V. watched over me like a hawk and made it clear to me that I had better stay away from those "cunts"! He referred to girls and women as "cunts" routinely. Till this day I find that word to be one of the nastiest words that can be uttered.

"During this time there were a lot of children hanging out at the rectory. Father had formed a basketball team, which included most of the boys I had grown up with in the parish. Some of them had never really attended the church, they had only attended the parish school. However, after Fr. V. became pastor of St. Charles Lwanga, many of them started coming to church and eventually began hanging around the rectory.

"Other boys now were getting keys to the rectory. I, of course, already had keys to everything. Eventually many of the other boys knew the codes to get into the keypad lock to Father V's suite.

"I noticed all kinds of things going on. I was not Father V's only plaything. One of the boy's father would often come to the door in the middle of the night. Fr. Stewart had known this man long before he came to St. Charles Lwanga. Fr. Stewart told me on several occasions that this man, Mr. N was on drugs. On one occasion, I went into Father's room and saw him and Mr. N having sex. They saw me, but said nothing. It was very traumatic to see this man who was a known drug user over Fr. V. having sex with him anally. I went down to my room traumatized and frightened. Thinking that Fr. V. would be angry with me, I tossed and turned all night expecting him to burst in my room. The next day there was a new latch on Fr. Stewart's door that he could slide to lock from the inside. We never talked about this incident, but we knew it was another secret we had between us.

"Oddly enough, and I learned later in life, I was to feel something that was consistent with this type of abuse. When I saw other kids in Fr. V.'s room I got a little jealous. That didn't last. Later I began to feel good about it, knowing it was somebody else's turn and not me. Boys going up to his room was like a revolving door. His appetite was insatiable! Some days he would have 4-5 boys come to his room at different times throughout the day. I always knew when there was something going on when he had the "latch" pulled on his door from the inside so I could not get in. This "latch" would forever tell the story as long as we lived in the same house. I remember the relief I began to feel when it was someone else other than me. In my adult years, the guilt of feeling happy that other boys were occupying his time instead of me weighed on me. Even though I know I was not happy to know they were being abused, I was just happy it wasn't me at that time. The older I got the more I hoped that someone each day would be around to fill his appetite so I would not have to be a course on that day.

"When I began to get interested in girls I would be in for more trouble. The first test was a girl who was related to one of his god sons who had come with him from one of his previous parishes. It is important to know that all of the boys at some point were called his god sons. I alone held the title of his son. She was in eighth grade and I was a freshman in high school, and of course I had very limited experience with girls. She would sneak to my room in the rectory regularly and we would fool around. We began to secretly date and it was wonderful. I felt *normal*. We wrote love letters to each other. She was sexual and raunchy with me and what teen-ager wouldn't like that. I hid her letters under my mattress and looked at them as treasures to be read whenever I needed a pick me up. Maybe the idea that our relationship was secret made it more thrilling, but in any case I liked it. As I got older I often wondered if she had been abused because her knowledge of "sexual acts" and the things she wrote to me were very mature. Being with her made me feel confident about my sexuality and with girls. I began to feel that no matter what I experienced at the hands of Fr. V., I ultimately knew who I was and I knew I was not gay! I knew what I felt with her was passion and a desire. I knew I never had this with Fr. V., no matter what he told me, bought me or threatened me with.

"One day when I came home from school Fr. V. was standing in my room with his face contorted in anger. I was familiar with his anger. Holding up a batch of letters he said, 'What the fuck is this?'

"I started crying. I knew my new girlfriend was over and my heart dropped.

"He was bristling. 'You are mine,' he snapped. 'Don't forget it.' 'You better leave that cunt alone'! At some point during this rant he slapped me in my face to ensure I got the point. There was no mistaking his meaning or his determination.

"I wasn't to have a girlfriend again for four years. I would see girls and talk to girls secretly. I was sexually active during these years, however I was very careful to ensure that Fr. V. did not find out about my activities. For four more years I would be trapped in a sexuality that was not of my own choosing but of someone else's. This made me feel less than human, like some plaything to amuse a particular man.

"About my junior year of high school the sexual abuse began to diminish, whether it was because he was losing his appetite or because he was having other boys. Whichever it was I was grateful. By diminish I mean the sex went from every day, to three times a week through the end of my junior year of high school. This may seem unusual because a kid this age and size should be able to fend off an abuser. Except that I was in his control, body, mind and soul. Again, I felt good when it was someone else other than me.

"Another odd part of my thinking was my psyche considered him my abuser, *but my father as well.* The ambivalence was painful, as someone who was supposed to love me also made me feel used."

"I wound up in counseling with a psychologist who was, a friend of Father V's. The psychologist, Dr. J is now an ordained Methodist priest. During this time I was transferred to Willibrord Catholic High School where my grades continued to plummet. The theme of my therapy with Dr. J was my relationship with my mother. I wonder if this was part of a conspiracy against me. After all, Dr. J was a good friend of Fr. V. He certainly wouldn't want to get Fr. V. into any kind of trouble. And so this professional, in the name of friendship, or maybe more, could not create a safe, trusting environment between us. By this time my hatred for my mother had increased because I blamed her for 'giving' me to Fr. V. During therapy I talked about the feelings I had for my mother, but I said that I was angry towards her because I felt she loved my brother more than me. Although some of that was true, I to some degree considered that natural feelings that some siblings have growing up. My mother and I had one joint session together and I remember feeling that she should know what's happening to me! I never disclosed anything about my abuse during my sessions. As I reflect back, there were a few times I considered telling Dr. J about the abuse. However, having been controlled and manipulated by Fr. V. for so long, depending on him as my provider/parent and Dr. J being a friend of his all chased those moments quickly away. After a year of therapy Dr. J told me 'there's nothing wrong with you. If you don't let go of the anger you have inside, it will control you and prevent you from being successful' This advice though simple hit me like a ton of bricks. A light bulb turned on inside of me. I made a commitment to myself to succeed. I decided to not let this abuse define me. I from that moment locked the abuse somewhere inside of me and compartmentalized what Fr. V. was doing to me.

At this point in the inquest I was asked again, not to editorialize, but to simply state the facts. I again told Dr. Bland that it was my story and I will tell it to my satisfaction. I reminded him that I have lived alone with this pain and that if I was going to tell the story, I was going to tell it all. After all, at this point, it was me against the Archdioceses of Chicago.

I went on. A question was asked why did I disclose anything to Dr. J and I replied, "No, if you mean did I tell Dr. J about the abuse, I did not". At this point, I wouldn't even consider getting Fr. V. in trouble. He was my father. When I needed lunch money, he gave it to me. My first car, he gave it to me. When I was sick, he took me to the doctor. Our secrets at this point were locked within our hearts and minds.

"During my junior year in high school Father wrote me a card. It said that I was a gift from God and that it caused him to grow more than heaven could before. He went on to say that he loved me like a father and that our relationship needed to change. This was in 1986. I wondered if this was really the end of it. Would I, at last, have my freedom, the right to choose my own sexuality, my own life?

"The sex abuse went way down. From three times a week to two times in a six month period. The anal sex stopped. Now it was only oral sex. Now I was able to see girls, and Father seemed to ignore them. He never endorsed a relationship with a girl and he would get angry if they called the phone for me.

He got me a car, keeping in the role of my guardian.

One night I had gone out and I believe I had a curfew of 11:00 pm. I went to see a girl I had grown up with when I lived in the Wentworth Gardens Housing Project. She had her own apartment on the south side of Chicago. But he wasn't really over the idea of my going out with girls, or, I suspect, anyone else. One night I stayed out late and was confronted by Fr. V. when I returned to the rectory. He asked me where I had been? I replied out. He repeated the question as he stood there in his white underwear and white tee shirt. I gave the same answer and then Fr. V. hit me hard across my face. I knew Father K had to hear the commotion, however as with his previous failures he ignored it. Enraged, his fists bunched, Fr. V. kneed me in the groin. As I went down he continued to hit me until I was pretty well beat up with a black eye. He kept muttering, 'Are you out with those bitches?' Later he tried to clean up my wounds with hydrogen peroxide."

During the inquest everybody listened to my story with seeming interest. Of course I had no way of knowing how sincere any of them were, especially the representatives of the Archdiocese.

This was at the height of the Church priest scandals and there were stories coming out of every part of the country. The Church was in denial and, beyond some rhetoric, didn't seem to really side with the victims, but looked at the whole problem as though it would be something that would go away soon.

But it wasn't going away and when people like me were making claims years later, many times with the abuser deceased or incapacitated, the charge was hurled that we were exploiters trying to capitalize on the Church's problems.

That's an insulting accusation, because such a notion was the last thing on my mind. Rather, what I hoped to convey by the way I related my story was to show how a young boy can be used, exploited and abused without even knowing it. In some ways I liken it to a woman raped by someone close to her. It is too hurtful to even speak about it to anyone else, let alone bring the abuser to justice. So, as in my own case, the great majority of these crimes are never reported. Therefore, when you consider the number that *have* been reported, the implications are staggering.

The fact that my abuser is now deceased doesn't make the abuse and the harm done to my life any less damaging. The hurt has been deep and lasting. Yet I refuse to let it consume me. I prefer to learn from this harsh life lesson, doing whatever I can to help abused kids and ease their suffering.

The Continuation

On April 13, 2006 I sat down with Dr. Stafford Henry in his downtown office on West Madison. I found myself in a chair that I had seen many children and parents in my 17 year career in Child Welfare sit in. I was meeting with a Psychologist who was looking to assess my every word. He would be waiting for me to share with him a story that I had only told to the Archdiocese of Chicago in the December 5, 2005 meeting. His office looked typical of a clinician. Everything was in place. The office was perfectly neat. His dress was none threatening and did not bring attention to himself. After he went through the template of why we were together, I began to tell the same story I shared on December 5, 2005. It felt good to tell the story again. Being an educated clinician I knew I needed this. The meeting went easier than when I first told the story to the Archdiocese of Chicago. Afterwards I thought about those who had been abused and were still afraid to come forward. I believe it was on that day that I decided I wanted to do more than just have the diocese acknowledge my abuse. I decided that I wanted to fight to take the "secrecy" out of the power that sexual predators have. The way we must fight pedophiles is we must like Dateline and Oprah, give them no place to hide. We must truly expose the secrets of their trade in order to have them identified out in the open so we know who they are. I would forsake the quiet nature in which my settlement was reached and publish the story for all to see. I would expose Fr. Stewart and his manipulative tools so that parents would know what to look for and better protect all children from the predator beast of a pedophile. Fr. Stewart could have been stopped if only adults would not have given him the constant benefit of "unsupervised" trust. We can beat the pedophile if we commit to it as a society. It can start with the Church becoming a leader and adopt a true zero tolerance for abuse. Of course the pedophile should be removed from ministry and prosecuted. However, if it is discovered that other clergy knew and assisted in a cover up in the abuse of children, they should also be removed and prosecuted as an accessory to the crime. Such a policy as mentioned previously would effectively snuff out the practice of clergy in the Church protecting it's own even when it is evident they have hurt others.

The last meeting I had prior to my settlement was the meeting in which I felt the most respected and heard. You would think that I would have felt this way in my meeting on December 5, 2005 when I met with representatives from the Assistance Ministry Office. As I mentioned previously, I felt disregarded and disrespected by Dr. Bland. It is my understanding he is no longer in that capacity anymore which is the best decision for all. He was not understanding and he from the start wanted to rush the interview. It was as if he did not want detail to be placed in the record. He is hopefully the "past" approach from that office. It is my hope that the new leadership in this office will see their role as not only fact finders, but of compassionate listeners. Not having felt good about the first meeting with the diocese I was not looking forward to the mediation meeting set for Wednesday, May 3, 2006 at the Law Offices of Burke, Warren, Mackay & Serritella, P.C. located in the IBM Plaza Building on North Wabash in Downtown Chicago. At this meeting with Dick Hawkins mediator, Jim Serritella, Head Attorney, Pat Carlson, lawyer from Burke, Warren Mackay & Serritella and my attorney Phillip Aaron. Being in a room full of lawyers I was sure that the environment would be uncomfortable and tense. From the beginning it was evident that the folks sitting around the table wanted to hear my story and was ready for the truth and was prepared to listen for as long as it took for the story to be told. I was especially impressed by the compassion that seemed to be in the questions and facial expressions of Jim Serritella. Jim listened patiently and asked questions that were not judging and none threatening. I had brought pictures taken when Fr. Stewart and I would go on various vacations, they looked through the pictures with interest and asked questions. I also provided documentation of a joint account with Fr. Stewart, report card from Lewis University where the rectory address was my official address, pictures I took of him and his mother, prom day pictures at the rectory and various other documentation. They looked through everything. The mediator Dick Hawkins would have to be one of the best in the business. He kept the room comfortable and remarked after the meeting that he had never had anyone lay out the story and cycle of the abuse as I did. I remarked that "I just told the truth". I think it amazes people when I can talk about accountability without hating Fr. Stewart. I hate Fr. Stewart's actions to me and the countless other children he victimized. I will never defend him for that and he has surely been judged by God. Fr. Stewart had a problem and could have been stopped. I forgive him for the pain he has caused to me. I however think our challenge is to not let pedophiles like Fr. Stewart go unchecked no matter what entity they represent. Please remember that the Church is the PEOPLE. If the Church has failed it has been able to do so because as the Church we the PEOPLE have not been good stewards in demanding that our leadership behave and respond the way we want them to. Hopefully my story will help call us all together as Church and as a society.

From Abused to Protector

Abuse began shortly before picture.
Kenneth in middle standing, Fr. Stewart sitting. First picture age 13 at Six Flags, Great America Amusment Park in Gurnee, IL.

Ken Sr & Mom in Rectory after 8th Grade Graduation, 1983. Where I was living at this time. Abuse already begun.

My Abuser and Parent
Fr. Victor E. Stewart

From Abused to Protector

Sexual abuse victims seek apology

BY KIMBERLY S. WETZEL
JULY 13, 2005

Growing up on Chicago's South Side, Monte Murphy and his brothers found a mentor in Father Victor Stewart, a priest at the now-closed St. Charles Lwanga Church.

No one paid much attention to the amount of time Stewart spent with the boys. In fact, the boys were just happy a father figure took an interest in them. Occasionally, Stewart took them to a movie or bought them things.

Murphy, now 35, says he was in sixth or seventh grade when Stewart began sexually abusing him. It lasted for several years.

It wasn't until a year and a half ago that Murphy learned his brothers, Reggie and Emanuel Murphy and London Lyons, were victims as well. The news broke his heart.

"We were preyed on because we were poor," Murphy said, "because we were young, because we were vulnerable."

Now, Murphy says, he suffers from nightmares and he and his brothers wrestle with drinking problems. His relationship with his wife is strained, and he struggles to trust people. He knows his problems stem from the abuse.

"It's difficult for me still," he said. "It distorts your mind and makes you confused."

Murphy and other alleged victims of sexual abuse by Stewart asked the Archdiocese of Chicago Wednesday to apologize and publicly admit it covered up sexual abuse. They also asked other victims to come forward.

The requests come amidst a firestorm of accusations against the Archdiocese of Chicago and several other Catholic

"IF WE CARE ENOUGH WE CAN MAKE A DIFFERENCE"

Medill News Service : Chicago

organizations throughout the country of covering up and fostering sexual abuse by priests. Last month, the Archdiocese of Chicago released two priests from the clergy who had been accused of abuse.

At a news conference outside the headquarters of the Chicago Archdiocese, Barbara Blaine, the president of the Survivors Network of Those Abused by Priests, called on the church to reach out to victims of priest abuse.

"These men have been suffering from years of embarrassment and shame," Blaine said. "[Stewart] molested these boys and shattered their innocence. The silence from the archdiocese is deafening. All this time, they have not taken any affirmative steps to reach out to other victims."

Several victims who attended the news conference told their stories with shaky voices and hands. Some were emotional; all were shy. They held up large pictures of Stewart and themselves as boys.

Derek Owens, 34, said he was abused by Stewart while he was an altar boy at St. Charles. He said he looked up to the priest and felt betrayed when the abuse started.

"This man was like the President to us," Owens said. "He was everything.

Your talking about poor kids who didn't have dads around. This guy was a father to a lot of us."

Stewart was an African-American priest who worked at St. Charles and St.

Ailbe churches as a priest, associate priest and boys basketball coach for several years before his death in 1994. Most of his victims were African-American boys.

Phillip Aaron, an attorney who represents Owens, the Murphys and several others who said they were abused by Stewart, said the priest knew how to gain the trust of the young boys by buying them sneakers and other things.

"He went through entire families sometimes," Aaron said.

Aaron, who helped 14 abuse victims settle with the archdiocese for more than

http://mesh.medill.northwestern.edu/mnschicago/archives/2005/07/snap_monte_m

$3 million in 2004, currently represents 20 more clients who say they were abused by Stewart. He said he is frustrated with the archdiocese's apparent lack of apology or taking responsibility for Stewart's and other abusive priests' actions, and the lack of initiative in seeking out other victims. He accused the archdiocese of covering up other instances of abuse.

Jim Dwyer, director of media relations for the Archdiocese of Chicago, called Aaron's and Blaine's accusations unfair.

"We're surprised by the statements made today because we don't think they're accurate," Dwyer said. "We have done more to address this issue than any other profession."

Dwyer denied that the archdiocese covered up any wrongdoing. He said members of the clergy have been working with Aaron's clients and providing counseling and interim financial assistance to the victims.

He pointed to the Archdiocese of Chicago's website – which provides information for victims and their families, including how to get counseling, how to report instances of abuse and a toll-free number to call – as an example of how the organization is reaching out.

"We ask people to come forward," Dwyer said. "We don't have the time or the resources to keep beating the bushes waiting for victims to come out. And I think it's unreasonable that people would ask that of us."

Dwyer said Aaron has never before asked for an apology on behalf of his clients, and the archdiocese has acknowledged problems with abuse through settlements and communication with Aaron and his clients.

"We have been talking to them," Dwyer said. "I would call that acknowledgement."

CBS 2 Chicago WBBM-TV: Men Want To Know If Alleged Abusive Priest Had HIV

Local News

© Jul 12, 2005 4:44 pm US/Central

Men Want To Know If Alleged Abusive Pr
Victims Request Priest's Medical Records

Joanie Lum
Reporting

(CBS) CHICAGO There are disturbing new allegations against a deceased Catholic priest from Chicago. Men who say they were sexually assaulted by him, believe he may have passed on a sexually transmitted disease to them.

Now, they're demanding answers.

The new allegations go beyond sexual abuse. The men say the former priest may have had AIDS and now they want to know his cause of death. CBS 2's Joanie Lum has more on the disturbing details.

"I was sexually abused by Father Stewart for a 10-year period," alleged abuse victim Reggie Murphy said.

Half a dozen men publicly accused a man they trusted and considered a father figure. Reverend Victor Stewart was a priest of the Chicago archdiocese during the 1980s and '90s and was exalted in their eyes.

Alleged abuse victim Derrick Owens said, "This man was in our life, he was like the president."

http://cbs2chicago.com/local/local_story_194175241.html   8/6/2005

From Abused to Protector

The men knew each other as boys growing up on the South Side, attending St. Charles Lwanga School -- which is now called Garfield School. The church at Garfield and Wentworth is no longer there.

They played on the basketball team that Father Stewart coached. They say they didn't know they had the same secret until they were adults, and their contact with Father Victor Stewart still haunts them.

"I'm 35 years old. I have dreams – nightmares; a hard time communicating with people," said alleged abuse victim Monty Murphy.

"It made me afraid to go back to school. I dropped out at a young age," said alleged abuse victim Troy Byrd.

They spoke outside the Chicago archdiocese headquarters and demanded the Church extend counseling to them and other victims. Their attorney wants the archdiocese to disclose the cause of Stewart's death. Stewart died in 1994.

"At the time of his death, he was frail and weak, the typical profile of an AIDS victim," victims' attorney Phillip Aaron said. "We want to know whether he had AIDS."

A spokesman for the Chicago archdiocese says the Church has helped the victims with both financial assistance and pastoral outreach. He says there was no indication that Father Stewart had AIDS. It was determined he died of complications following surgery for a subdural hematoma.

(© MMV, CBS Broadcasting, Inc. All Rights Reserved.)

SPONSORED

The Inquest

Chicago Tribune news: Church urged to find other abuse victims

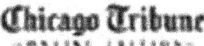

http://www.chicagotribune.com/news/local/chicago/chi-0507140240jul14,1,4556416,story?page=1&coll=chi-newslocalchicago-hed

Church urged to find other abuse victims

Priest who has died named in 22 cases

By Margaret Ramirez
Tribune religion reporter

July 14, 2005

African-American men who were sexually abused as children by a Roman Catholic priest demanded Wednesday that church officials take steps to find other victims who may be suffering in silence.

Rev. Victor Stewart, who died in 1994 at age 54, abused at least 22 boys during the 1980s, some as young as 7, according to an attorney for the accusers.

Fourteen of the men have reached settlements totaling $3 million with the Archdiocese of Chicago, said attorney Phillip Aaron of Seattle. Settlements are pending for eight more victims, he said.

Stewart, an African-American priest, worked at two South Side parishes—St. Charles Luanga, now closed, and St. Ailbe—as pastor, principal and basketball coach, victims said.

Archdiocese spokesman Jim Dwyer confirmed that church officials had reached a settlement with Stewart's accusers but declined to provide details. Their claims were determined to be credible, he said.

Speaking out publicly for the first time Wednesday, several victims said Stewart preyed on families who were struggling financially, showering the children with gifts and then abusing them.

Monty Murphy, 35, said that when he told his younger brother, Reggie, two years ago about the abuse, he learned the priest had molested them both.

"We have cried many nights together about this," said Murphy, one of about 10 victims of Stewart who attended a news conference outside archdiocese headquarters. "When you're young and innocent, you don't know why this is happening."

"I have nightmares," Murphy said as his voice cracked. "I still have difficulty understanding why this happened to me."

http://www.chicagotribune.com/news/local/chicago/chi-0507140240jul14,1,3792505,print... 7/15/200

"IF WE <u>CARE ENOUGH</u> WE CAN MAKE A DIFFERENCE" 23

Aaron provided settlement documents, dated 2003, stating that Stewart "allegedly took or committed unwanted sexual actions" with minors, resulting in personal and physical injuries, and church officials "failed to take reasonable steps to prevent such conduct."

He said he believes there are more victims who have not spoken.

"This man was a serial predator, a serial pedophile who preyed on African-American young males," Aaron said. "And there has not been any effort by the archdiocese to come forward and find more victims.

"You have to wonder what type of church this is. Where is the humanity in this?"

Aaron also said several of the victims contracted sexually transmitted diseases from Stewart, and they were concerned that he may have had AIDS.

"At the time of his death, he had the typical profile of an AIDS victim," said Aaron.

Dwyer said the cause of Stewart's death on June 10, 1994, was a subdural hematoma, a bleeding on the surface of the brain.

"We have no reason to believe he had AIDS," Dwyer said. "He died of complications from a surgery he had June 1, shortly before he died."

Asked why the archdiocese had not released a statement on Stewart's abusive past, Dwyer said archdiocese policy is to make an official statement only when an accused priest is removed or withdrawn from active ministry.

Dwyer also said the archdiocese would not make efforts to find other victims.

"He has been dead for more than 10 years. We don't have the unlimited resources to do this," said Dwyer. "If someone is dead, how can you possibly make a complete determination of the abuse?"

Victims' advocates have asked archdiocese officials to post names of all abusive priests on its Web site, but the request has been refused. Dwyer said any person seeking information on a particular priest can make a request on the Web site—or by mail, phone or fax.

Several other dioceses, including Baltimore, Los Angeles, Milwaukee, Tucson, Ariz., and Spokane, Wash., have disclosed on their Web sites the names of priests who have faced credible abuse allegations.

"Father Stewart molested these boys and shattered their innocence," said Barbara Blaine, president and founder of the Survivors Network of those Abused by Priests. "At the minimum, the archdiocese should publicly acknowledge that Victor Stewart abused children."

As of last month, the Archdiocese of Chicago had received 63 credible allegations since January 2002 o priests abusing minors. Of the 28 priests accused, seven are dead, 10 were withdrawn from ministry, 10 resigned and one is incarcerated. Last year, the Chicago Archdiocese spent $18.2 million to resolve sex abuse claims.

Troy Byrd, who said he was abused by Stewart at age 8, said names of abusive priests should be available to the public regardless of whether the abuser was living or dead.

Chicago Tribune news: Church urged to find other abuse victims

"He made me afraid to go to school," said Byrd. "Now, this is the best thing I can do to prevent this fro happening to other children."

----

maramirez@tribune.com

Copyright © 2005, Chicago Tribune

HOME | NEWS | MONEY | SPORTS | ENTERTAINMENT | FEATURES

NEWS

Chicago: Things to know

July 14, 2005

Lefkow returns to bench

U.S. District Judge Joan Humphrey Lefkow made a low-key return to the bench, just months after the murders of her husband and mother. She had vowed she would continue working despite the Feb. 28 shootings at her North Side home, committed by a man upset with her decision to dismiss his medical malpractice lawsuit. Tuesday, a notice posted on the door of her courtroom at the Dirksen U.S. Courthouse thanked people for their sympathy and asked them to refrain from mentioning the deaths during court proceedings. The judge appeared relaxed in court where she presided over several routine civil cases. She plans to continue on the bench on a limited basis the next several months.

New park on former UIC site

The Chicago Park District board OK'd a new park at Sangamon and Adams near Greektown. The 1.4-acre lot is currently the site of a five-story building used for storage by UIC. Using $7.3 million in state and city dollars, the district will buy the land from the university and demolish the building. A community planning process will decide what amenities might be included. District spokesman Arnold Randall said many industrial buildings in the area have been converted to residential creating a demand for open space.

Priest's victims paid $3M

The Archdiocese of Chicago paid over $3 million to 14 people who claim they were sexually abused by the late Rev. Victor Stewart, pastor, principal and basketball coach at St. Charles Lwanga and St. Ailbe on the South Side. There are at least eight more victims and 20 more potential victims, attorney Philip Aaron said. Survivors Network of Those Abused By Priests President Barbara Blaine accused the Archdiocese of turning a blind eye to the abuse and failing to reach out to victims, now in their 20s and 30s.

http://www.chicagoredstreak.com/news/mid-news-midchbrf141.html   8/6/2005

ARCHDIOCESE OF CHICAGO

Office of Professional Responsibility

P.O. Box 1979
Chicago, Illinois 60690-1979

(312) 751-5205
Fax: (312) 751-5279
www.archchicago.org

February 27, 2006

Mr. Kenneth Joe
C/o Mr. Phillip Aaron
4020 East Madison
Suite 200
Seattle, WA 98112

Dear Mr. Joe,

Enclosed you will find a finalized report of your allegation dated December 5, 2005 with the changes you submitted.

Upon your review of the report, please provide your signature and date and return the document in the envelope provided.

Mr. Joe, in the interest of continuing to expedite this process, I ask that you return the enclosed report to this office by March 13, 2006. In the event that we do not receive any response from you by March 13, 2006, we will assume that the final report is accurate.

If you have any questions, please feel free to contact Patty Zacharias at 312-867-8793.

Sincerely,

Laura A. Neri-Palomino

Laura A. Neri-Palomino
Administrative Assistant

Enclosure

**Report From Meeting with
Archdiocese of Chicago**

"IF WE <u>CARE ENOUGH</u> WE CAN MAKE A DIFFERENCE"

ARCHDIOCESE OF CHICAGO

Office of Professional Responsibility

P.O. Box 2278
Chicago, Illinois 60690-2078

(312) 751-5205
Fax (312) 751-5279
www.archchicago.org

Memorandum

To: File – PFR-39

From: Patricia Zacharias, Professional Responsibility Assistant Administrator

Re: Allegations of Sexual Misconduct of a Minor Against Rev. Victor Stewart (Deceased) Made by Mr. Kenneth Joe (formerly Nolan)

Date: February 27, 2006

Please note that all corrections and additions to the December 5, 2005 report made by Mr. Joe are in bold and italicized.

Date of Meeting: December 5, 2005   **Time of Meeting:** 3 PM

Present at Meeting:
Mr. Kenneth Joe
Attorney Phillip Aaron
~~Mr. Richie Aaron, Paralegal for Attorney Phillip Aaron~~ *not present*
Dr. Michael Bland, Assistance Ministry
Ms. Patricia Zacharias, Professional Responsibility Assistant Administrator (PRAA)

In-Person Meeting:
Mr. Joe, Attorney Phillip Aaron and Mr. Richie Aaron, Paralegal for the Office of Attorney Phillip Aaron arrived at the Archdiocese of Chicago office for the scheduled 3:00 PM meeting. Dr. Bland and Ms. Zacharias (PRAA) joined them.

As the meeting began, PRAA explained her role in taking notes as Mr. Joe talked and preparing the draft of the report afterwards. Dr. Bland's role in being there for support *and to help the Archdiocese services regarding counseling if needed* was also explained.

Ms. Zacharias gave Mr. Joe an envelope with information pertaining to the Illinois Department of Children and Family Services and the State's Attorney's Office. He was also provided with a copy of the Archdiocese of Chicago policy: §1100 *Sexual Abuse of Minors: Policies for Education, Prevention, Assistance to Victims and Procedures for Determination of Fitness for Ministry*. Ms. Zacharias explained that Attorney Aaron is familiar with the information and could review it with Mr. Joe if he would like.

Report From Meeting with Archdiocese of Chicago

The Inquest

Allegation – PFR-39
December 5, 2005
Page 2

PRAA asked Mr. Joe to begin where he felt most comfortable in regards to his allegation of sexual abuse against Fr. Victor Stewart. She explained she might have some clarification questions at the end to ensure she captures the information correctly. Mr. Joe stated:

- "I've tried to put this behind me for many years. The times I did try to deal with it, I did not receive any assistance, so I had to not deal with it."
- Mr. Joe met with Fr. ███████ who told him to pray about it. He met with called ███████ the Vicar for Priests at the time who talked to him on the phone and "nothing." This was around the time Fr. Stewart got sick.
- ███████████████████████████████████████ worked in child welfare for 16 years. I've never talked in this type of detail, not even to my wife."
- Mr. Joe met Fr. Stewart before Fr. got installed. This was sometime in 1982. Mr. Joe was in seventh grade and was aware that Fr. Stewart was coming to St. Charles Lwanga. Mr. Joe felt excited because he knew Fr. Stewart was a black priest. The former priests, Fr. Burke and Fr. Backus were good priests, but it would be good to have a black priest. *(The records from the Archdiocesan archives state Fr. Stewart was the Pastor of St Charles Lwanga Parish from 9/23/82 – 7/1/90.)*
- Mr. Joe remembers the first time he met Fr. Stewart; Fr. had been standing on the church school steps. Fr. was not wearing his collar, so Mr. Joe did not know he was a priest. Fr. Stewart asked Mr. Joe, "Who are you?" Mr. Joe replied, "I am Kenneth F. Nolan and who are you?" Fr. Stewart then explained who he was. Fr. was with ███████.
- Fr. Stewart began reaching out to Mr. Joe to "hang-out."
- Fr. Stewart had some of his Godsons from other parishes living with him at the rectory of St. Charles Lwanga. Some of these boys/men included ███████ (who committed suicide later on in his life), ███████████████████████.
- Another young man by the name of ███████ told Mr. Joe, "I used to be you." This seemed to mean that he used to be special to Fr. Stewart, as he now perceived Mr. Joe to be.
- Mr. Joe spent time with these boys/young men and Fr. Stewart. They would go bowling. He was the only "child" in the group and was about age 12 at the time.
- Mr. Joe described growing up in the projects with very little money. His mother could not afford to take them bowling. Their refrigerator was frequently empty.
- Fr. Stewart began buying Mr. Joe gifts around Christmastime, 1982.
- These gifts included video games such as Frogger and Donkey Kong and a portable television set. Mr. Joe belonged to a family of eight members and remembers there was some jealousy among his family members about the gifts he was receiving.
- The first incident of abuse occurred sometime between July and September 1982. It was not cold outside. At this time, Fr. Stewart had been taking him to Ford City Shopping Center to buy him clothes. This is also where they went

Report From Meeting with Archdiocese of Chicago

"IF WE CARE ENOUGH WE CAN MAKE A DIFFERENCE"

Allegation – PFR-39
December 5, 2000
Page 3

bowling. Prior to this, Mr. Joe had only been to Evergreen Plaza. He recalls Fr. Stewart taking him to the Gap clothing store and buying him corduroy pants in every color available.

- Mr. Joe "craved" for a positive male relationship in his life. His father was not there. He was around but not on a regular basis.
- Mr. Joe had just started the school year when the first incident of abuse took place. The day before, Fr. Stewart had taken Mr. Joe shopping. On this particular day, Mr. Joe and Fr. Stewart were sitting in the TV room within the rectory. The TV room was located on the second floor. It contained a big counsel television set and three black leather couches. The room was paneled and had a patio door leading to a screened-in patio. Mr. Joe and Fr. Stewart were sitting together on the medium couch.
- Fr. Stewart would always hug Mr. Joe when he saw him. Mr. Joe had been uncomfortable with this at the beginning of it. Fr. Stewart was now hugging him close on the couch. He then began unbuttoning Mr. Joe's shirt with the same arm that was hugging him. Fr. Stewart did not say anything. He began rubbing Mr. Joe's nipple. Mr. Joe got a "hard-on" for the first time from stimulation.
- Mr. Joe felt uncomfortable and did not know what was happening. He felt conflicted because he had begun to like Fr. Stewart.
- Fr. ███ who was an Associate Pastor at St. Charles Lwanga walked into the room. Fr. Stewart did not move his hand from within Mr. Joe's shirt. Fr. ███ and Fr. Stewart had a conversation together for about five minutes. Fr. ███ left and Fr. Stewart got up and locked the door. He then touched Mr. Joe's "private area." He did not take off any of Mr. Joe's clothes "yet." Prior to this incident, Mr. Joe had been spending the night at the rectory. Fr. Stewart would take him to a late movie and then call Mr. Joe's mother to obtain permission for him to spend the night there.
- This time Mr. Joe spent the night in Fr. Stewart's bedroom. Fr. Stewart took off Mr. Joe's clothes and looked at his body like it was art. Fr. had taken off all of his clothes with the exception of his underwear. Fr. Stewart then took off his underwear, picked up Mr. Joe and carried him to the bed. He laid Mr. Joe on the bed and then lay down next to him. Fr. Stewart began to kiss Mr. Joe as he stroked Mr. Joe's penis. Mr. Joe felt uncomfortable when Fr. Stewart tried to put his tongue in his mouth. Fr. Stewart sucked on Mr. Joe's nipples and Mr. Joe ejaculated for the first time. They then performed mutual oral sex on each other.
- Mr. Joe described feeling pissed off because that is how he lost his virginity.
- In January 1983, Mr. Joe moved into the rectory to live. Fr. Stewart's bedroom was now located on the third floor. Mr. Joe was the youngest boy in his family, but not the youngest child. There were numerous conflicts with his mother regarding her having to go to school because Mr. Joe was in trouble. His mother agreed to have Mr. Joe live with Fr. Stewart in the hopes that Fr. Stewart could help improve Mr. Joe's behavior at school. *This was what Father Stewart suggested.* (School records for Kenneth Nolan from the Archives of the Archdiocese of Chicago have copies of reports from a variety of school professionals describing various behavior problems. These reports are dated from 9/1981-1/83.)

**Report From Meeting with
Archdiocese of Chicago**

Allegation – PPR-39
December 5, 2005
Page 4

- Mr. Joe's room was on the second floor, which is the same floor Fr. ▓▓▓ room was on. Ms. ▓▓▓ was the housekeeper at the time. She was the mother of Fr. ▓▓▓. Mr. Joe remembers her as being mean. He believes she resented his being there at the rectory as he was the only child living there at the time.
- Mr. Joe "went everywhere" with Fr. Stewart. People generally thought Fr. Stewart had adopted Mr. Joe.
- The abuse had escalated to anal sex during this time. Mr. Joe slept in Fr. Stewart's bedroom and bed. Fr. Stewart would say to Mr. Joe, "You are my wife."
- Mr. Joe and Fr. Stewart took vows with each other one night when they were laying naked in bed together.
- Mr. Joe said he did not care about what was happening, that he was "fine at the moment."
- Mr. Joe then graduated from grammar school and continued to have school problems. The problems at school had started around the time the abuse began. He remembers being in the school office everyday. There was a two-month period where he did not go to school. The school would send homework to him, which he would do in bed *at the rectory. This was in 8th grade.*
- Mr. Joe always felt uncomfortable when Fr. Stewart would get mad at him due to *not performing right sexually* and be mean to him. He would have to sit on the first floor of the rectory and do his homework.
- There were days Fr. Stewart would tell him, "Don't get dressed." Fr. would then lock the door with a deadbolt. The housekeeper during this time ▓▓▓ did not have a key. Mr. Joe had a key to the *bathroom bedroom*.
- Fr. enrolled him in Quigley South Seminary acting as his guardian. Fr. was listed as his main contact person. Mr. Joe's mother was not listed anywhere.
- Mr. Joe felt angry with Quigley. He felt uncomfortable taking showers with the other boys. He felt uncomfortable having to meet with the other priests there. He believed they knew about his being abused by Fr. Stewart and that they too would abuse him.
- During this time there were many other children hanging around at the rectory. *Fr. Stewart formed a basketball team to include:* ▓▓▓
- ▓▓▓ families had not been attending church at St. Charles Lwanga until Fr. Stewart had become the pastor.
- Other boys began to also get keys to the rectory. Mr. Joe had keys to everything. Many of the other boys knew the codes to get into the keypad lock to Fr. Stewart's suite.
- ▓▓▓ father would come to the door in the middle of the night. On one occasion, Mr. Joe went into Fr. Stewart's room and observed Fr. Stewart and ▓▓▓ "having sex." He believes they saw him there, did not stop having sex and it was never discussed. The next day there was a new latch on Fr. Stewart's door.
- Mr. Joe felt some jealousy when Fr. Stewart had other children in his room with him and had the door latched so Mr. Joe could not enter. *However, Mr. Joe began to feel good when there was someone else in the room.*

**Report From Meeting with
Archdiocese of Chicago**

Allegation – PFR-39
December 5, 2006
Page 5

- Mr. Joe began to secretly date a girl by the name of ▓▓▓▓▓ who was related to ▓▓▓▓▓. He had letters to and from her hidden under his mattress. He remembers her as very sexual and raunchy with him. ▓▓▓▓▓ in 6th grade and ▓▓ he was a freshman at the time.
- One day, Fr. Stewart approached him with a bag of letters and asked him, "What the fuck is this?"
- Mr. Joe began crying and Fr. Stewart slapped him, telling him, "You are mine."
- Mr. Joe then knew he could not have a girlfriend or Fr. Stewart would hurt him. So he did not have a girlfriend for the next four years. *Father made him end the relationship.*
- Around this time, the sexual abuse became less frequent. The frequency had changed from "everyday to three times a week through the end of the junior year of high school." Mr. Joe felt some relief when he saw someone else going upstairs instead of him. He knew he would then probably be safe for the night. He saw Fr. Stewart as his abuser and as his father.
- He was put into counseling with a psychologist by the name of ▓▓▓▓▓. Mr. ▓▓▓▓▓ is now an ordained Methodist priest.
- During this time, Mr. Joe transferred to ▓▓▓▓▓ Willibrord Catholic High School. His grades were all failing. The focus of his therapy with ▓▓▓▓▓ was his relationship with his mother. Mr. ▓▓▓▓▓ was a personal friend of Fr. Stewart. Mr. Joe hated his mother at the time *for giving him to Father Stewart.* During their last therapy session ▓▓▓▓▓ told Mr. Joe that "There is nothing wrong with you, do not let your anger destroy you." Mr. Joe recalls making a personal decision for himself at that point to not let his anger bring him down. *Mr. Joe was afraid to tell* ▓▓ *about the abuse.*
- Mr. Joe described Fr. Stewart trying to "do right" by him. During his junior year in high school, Fr. Stewart wrote him a card. In the card, Fr. said that Mr. Joe was a gift from God causing him to grow more than he ever has before. Fr. went on to write that he loved him like a ▓▓▓▓ *father* and their relationship needed to change. This occurred in 1986.
- The frequency of abuse now changed from three times a week to two times in a six-month period. The anal sex stopped. The abuse consisted of oral sex and ejaculation. Mr. Joe believed Fr. Stewart was struggling to stop the abuse altogether. Mr. Joe began bringing girls around which Fr. Stewart would now allow but did not show much interest in.
- Fr. Stewart had a car signed under Mr. Joe's (Kenneth Nolan) name.
- Mr. Joe was now dating a woman by the name of ▓▓▓▓▓. She had her own apartment on ▓▓▓▓▓. One night he had stayed out late and was confronted by Fr. Stewart when he returned to the rectory. He told Fr. Stewart he had been at ▓▓▓▓▓. Fr. Stewart hit him ▓▓▓▓▓▓▓▓▓▓▓▓▓▓▓▓▓▓▓. It was loud and Mr. Joe believes Fr ▓▓▓ had to hear what was going on. Fr. Stewart "kneed" Mr. Joe in his "private parts." Fr. Stewart went on to beat him up including blackening his eye. Fr. Stewart was saying to him, "Are you out with those bitches?" After it was over, Fr. Stewart felt bad and tried to tend to Mr. Joe's wounds with hydrogen peroxide.

**Report From Meeting with
Archdiocese of Chicago**

The Inquest

Allegation – PFR-39
December 5, 2005
Page 6

- Mr. Joe went away to college in 1987. He attended Lewis University. He states a ███████████ attempted to abuse him there.
- There were two more episodes of abuse with Fr. Stewart between 1987-1990. These occurred when Mr. Joe returned to the rectory during college breaks or to do things like his laundry.
- Mr. Joe described his feelings currently about Fr. Stewart saying, "I loved him, I shouldn't have, I still do. I hate him for what he did. He destroyed my family."
- Mr. Joe remembers another boy named ███████████ living at the rectory for a short period of time.
- Mr. Joe's brother ████ moved into the rectory when Mr. Joe was a freshman in high school. It was during this time that ███████████ also moved in.
- During Mr. Joe's freshman year in high school he contracted "crabs." Fr. Stewart told him what it was and said he also had it. Fr. Stewart went to Walgreen's Drug Store and bought two kits. Mr. Joe cut off his hair and Fr. Stewart put "blue stuff" on both of them. He had to take all of his sheets off of his bed and gave them to Fr. Stewart. Mr. Joe said this is the only time he has ever had a sexually transmitted disease.
- St. Charles Lwanga closed between 1987-1991 and that is when the abuse ended.
- Mr. Joe could not move in to the rectory of St. Ailbe's Parish with Fr. Stewart. (The records from the Archdiocese archives indicate Fr. Stewart was a Pastor at St. Ailbe Parish from 7/1/90 – 10/8/92)
- Fr. Stewart got an apartment for Mr. Joe and his brother at 52nd and Drexel Streets in the Hyde Park area. This gave Mr. Joe a place to stay when he came home from college.
- Mr. Joe had Thanksgiving dinner and all other holidays at Fr. Stewarts' mothers house. He helped to take care of her before she passed away.
- Mr. Joe remembers being on the Archdiocesan payroll beginning his freshman year in high school. He was on a joint checking account with Fr. Stewart at *Heritage Pullbox Bank on 111th in Chicago.*
- Mr. Joe took care of Fr. Stewart when he was sick. Fr. Stewart could not remember things because of his strokes. The last time he saw Fr. Stewart was right before he went into his last "episode" of illness before he passed away. He brought ████, his college girlfriend with him.

There were three additional items which Mr. Joe wanted to emphasize were important for him to share:

1. ████ he and Fr. Stewart had a key to *the Church collection box* and he was in charge of the collection box. Fr. Stewart had him take $200.00 out of the collection every Sunday for four years.
2. Fr. ████ had to know about the abuse, which was going on because he lived there. There was also a Deacon ████ who lived there for a while. He then had an argument with Fr. Stewart and did not live there anymore. Mr. Joe chose not to go to priests such as Fr. ███████ or Fr. ███████ because of rumors from Fr. about their behavior with other men or boys.

**Report From Meeting with
Archdiocese of Chicago**

"IF WE CARE ENOUGH WE CAN MAKE A DIFFERENCE"   33

From Abused to Protector

Allegation – PFR-39
December 5, 2005
Page 7

3. "The Archdiocese of Chicago should be ashamed. There could not have possibly been a more motherfucking child molester within the Archdiocese of Chicago then Fr. Stewart. Some children were abused for one day, some for three months, and some for six months. There were at least 60 children abused at St. Charles Lwanga. I am coming forward because my brother got screwed up and for the others who are not as strong as I am. The priests knew."

Ms. Zacharias asked if there was anything else Mr. Joe would like to share at this time and Mr. Joe said there was not. Ms. Zacharias explained he would also have the opportunity to add more information upon his review of the draft of his allegation. Dr. Bland and Ms. Zacharias thanked Mr. Joe for all of the information he shared with them. It is to be noted that this report is intended only to provide a summary of information regarding the alleged sexual abuse by Fr. Victor Stewart shared by Mr. Kenneth Joe on December 5, 2005.

_____   _____3/22/06_____
Kenneth Joe   Date

_____   _____
Patricia Zacharias, Assistant Administrator   Date

_____   _____
Dr. Michael Bland, Assistance Ministry   Date

Cc: Rev. Daniel Smilanic, Cardinal's Delegate to the Review Board
Rev. Edward D. Grace, Vicar for Priests
Rev. Vince Costello, Vicar for Priests
Ralph Bonaccorsi, Assistance Ministry
Philip Aaron, Civil Attorney

Report From Meeting with Archdiocese of Chicago

"IF WE CARE ENOUGH WE CAN MAKE A DIFFERENCE"

The Inquest

THE LAW OFFICES OF PHILLIP AARON
ATTORNEY AT LAW

4020 EAST MADISON
SUITE 200
SEATTLE, WA 98112

TEL: (206) 323-4466
FAX: (206) 860-0564

April 24, 2006

Dear Mr. Joe:

You are scheduled to appear for your mediation on Wednesday May 3rd 2006 at 9:00am to be held at:

Burke, Warren, MacKay & Serritella, P.C.
22nd Floor, IBM Plaza
330 North Wabash Ave.
Chicago IL 60611

Please plan to stay the entire day. If applicable, your airfare or train schedule is attached. Hotel arrangements will be sent shortly.

Yours Truly,

Phillip Aaron

Phillip Aaron

Mediation Letter

"IF WE CARE ENOUGH WE CAN MAKE A DIFFERENCE"

SETTLEMENT AGREEMENT AND GENERAL RELEASE OF ALL CLAIMS

This Settlement Agreement ("Agreement") is hereby entered into as of _____, 2006, which is the date when the last signatory executes this Agreement (the "Effective Date"), by and between the Catholic Bishop of Chicago, a corporation sole (the "Catholic Bishop"), and Kenneth Joe ("Joe" or "Claimant") (collectively "the Parties").

WITNESSETH

WHEREAS, Kenneth Joe alleges that Rev. Victor E. Stewart ("Stewart"), who was at all relevant times a priest of the Archdiocese of Chicago, allegedly took or committed unwanted sexual actions with Kenneth Joe while he was a minor, which Joe alleges resulted in personal and physical injuries to him. Kenneth Joe further alleges that the Catholic Bishop and its agents failed to take reasonable steps to prevent such conduct or are otherwise liable for his injuries;

WHEREAS, Kenneth Joe was formerly known as "Kenneth Nolan", and is over eighteen (18) years of age, of sufficient mental ability to appreciate the effect of his action entering into this Agreement, and of legal age under the law of Illinois;

WHEREAS, the Catholic Bishop denies that it was negligent or that it otherwise caused or is liable for the injuries claimed by Joe;

WHEREAS, the Parties and each of them believe it is in their respective best interests to enter into this Agreement;

WHEREAS, the Parties intend to bring closure to the matter being resolved in this Agreement and from the date of this Agreement forward, to conduct themselves in a manner that is consistent with that intention;

WHEREAS, the amount paid to Kenneth Joe pursuant to this Agreement is intended to be and is in full and final satisfaction of any claims for personal, physical, and psychological injuries which he has made or may make against the Catholic Bishop or any instrumentality of the Catholic Church or their present or former directors, officers, members, clergy, bishops,

Settlement Page 1

priests, employees, volunteers, agents, attorneys, insurers, representatives, predecessors, successors, assigns, or affiliates; or against Rev. Victor E. Stewart or his successors or estate;

WHEREAS, all of the Parties hereto are represented by counsel and have had the opportunity to discuss this Agreement with counsel;

NOW, THEREFORE, in consideration of the foregoing premises and for other good and valuable consideration (the sufficiency of which is hereby acknowledged by each of the Parties), it is hereby covenanted and agreed by and between the Parties hereto as follows:

1. Payment. Within 30 days of the Effective Date, the Catholic Bishop shall pay to Kenneth Joe the sum of ~~[redacted]~~ by check made payable to the "Client Trust Account of Phillip Aaron."

2. Complete Release of Catholic Bishop and Rev. Victor E. Stewart. Kenneth Joe on his own behalf and on behalf of his current and future agents, employees, representatives, attorneys, successors and assigns hereby completely and unconditionally releases, discharges and waives all claims, damages, causes of action, debts, liabilities, torts, covenants, contracts, agreements, undertakings and other obligations of whatever nature or source, statutory or otherwise, whether known or unknown (including, without limitation, any claim for sexual abuse, personal injury, negligence, or breach of fiduciary duty, and any claim for attorney's fees and costs), arising out of any matter prior to the date of this Agreement, which he has, had or may have against the Catholic Bishop or any instrumentality of the Catholic Church or their present or former directors, officers, members, clergy, bishops, priests, employees, volunteers, agents, attorneys, insurers, representatives, predecessors, successors, assigns, or affiliates, or against Rev. Victor E. Stewart and his successors or estate. Kenneth Joe covenants and warrants that he has not assigned or transferred, or purported to assign or transfer, the claims released in this Agreement.

3. Binding. This Agreement shall be binding upon the Parties hereto and their respective successors in interest, heirs, personal representatives and assigns.

Settlement Page2

4. **No Admission of Wrongdoing.** Nothing contained in this Agreement, nor any action taken by any party in connection with this Agreement, constitutes an admission of wrongdoing or liability on the part of any party.

5. **Additional Documents.** The Parties shall execute, acknowledge and deliver to other parties such instruments or confirmation or other or further assurance after the date of the Agreement as may be reasonably required to carry out its purposes.

6. **Mediation and Arbitration.** The Parties shall in good faith use their best efforts to resolve all disputes arising out of this Agreement by mediation. The Parties shall endeavor to agree upon a Mediator within thirty (30) days of the date a party first notifies the other Parties of a desire to seek mediation. If the Parties are unable to agree upon a mediator within thirty (30) days, then in the thirty (30) days immediately following, each party shall select a party Mediator who in turn shall agree by consensus or majority vote (when there is a sufficient number of Parties) on an independent Mediator. The Mediator, or the party Mediators and the independent Mediator, shall conduct the mediation. If the mediation is not successful, the Mediator or Mediators shall certify the date on which the mediation failed.

If the mediation fails, the Parties may, but are not required to, agree to binding arbitration of the dispute. If the Parties agree to binding arbitration, then within fourteen (14) days of the date the mediation failed, the Mediator (or Mediators, acting unanimously) shall appoint an Arbitrator to conduct binding arbitration. If the Mediators are unable to unanimously agree upon an Arbitrator within fourteen (14) days of the date the mediation failed, then within the next seven (7) days following (a total of twenty-one (21) days from the date the mediation failed) each of the party Mediators shall appoint an Arbitrator and these arbitrators shall choose an additional impartial Arbitrator by consensus or at least a majority vote (when there is a sufficient number of Parties). The Arbitrator(s) shall schedule a hearing to occur within sixty (60) days of the date the mediation failed. The hearing may proceed thereafter as necessary. The Arbitrator(s) shall preside over the binding arbitration, shall have the authority to establish the rules and procedures that govern the arbitration, and shall have the power to decide any dispute

Settlement Page3

The Inquest

THE LAW OFFICES   PHILLIP AARON
ATTORNEY AT LAW

4020 EAST MADISON
SUITE 20
SEATTLE, WA 98111

TEL (206) 323-446
FAX: (206) 860-056

SETTLEMENT STATEMENT

TO: Kenneth Joe
RE: Joe v Stewart
DOL: 1976

GROSS AMOUNT RECEIVED PRO GENERAL RELEASE $ ■■■■■■

Disbursements

Outside advanced costs   ■■■■.00

Attorney Fees ($1/3 of $■■■■■■)   ■■■■■■

Total Disbursement & Fees $ ■■■■■■

TO CLIENT $ ■■■■■■

STATE OF WASHINGTON)
) SS
COUNTY OF KING   )

I, Kenneth Joe, being first duly sworn upon oath, deposes and says:

That I received the sum of Five Hundred Sixty Thousand Four Hundred Sixteen Dollars and Sixty-Seven Cents ($■■■■■■).

_____
KENNETH JOE

SCRIBED AND SWORN to before me this 22nd day of June, 2006

Settlement Page4   NOTARY PUBLIC in and for the
                      State of _____ residing at _____

"IF WE CARE ENOUGH WE CAN MAKE A DIFFERENCE"

To: Kenneth Joe
[Address]

With a copy to: Phillip Aaron
Suite 200
4020 East Madison Street
Seattle, WA 98112-3150

To: Catholic Bishop of Chicago, a corporation sole
Vicar for Priests Office
645 N. Michigan Avenue, Suite 543
Chicago, Illinois 60611

With a copy to: James A. Serritella, Esq.
Burke, Warren, MacKay & Serritella, P.C.
330 N. Wabash Avenue, 22nd Floor
Chicago, IL 60611-3607

If mailed, such notice shall be deemed delivered when deposited in the United States mail in a sealed envelope so addressed, with postage prepaid. If sent by facsimile or, such notice shall be deemed delivered when the facsimile is sent. If sent by overnight courier, such notice shall be deemed delivered when delivered to the overnight courier.

10. Laws of Illinois. This Agreement shall be construed in accordance with the laws of the State of Illinois, without reference to its choice of law provisions.

11. Severability. Any invalidity, in whole or in part, of any provision of this Agreement shall not affect the validity of any other of its provisions or of the Agreement as a whole.

12. Entire Agreement. This Agreement constitutes the entire agreement between the Parties. This Agreement may be amended only by a written instrument signed by all Parties.

13. Counterparts. This Agreement may be executed in counterparts.

14. Headings. Headings have been inserted for convenience of reference only. They are not intended to affect the meaning or interpretation of this Agreement.

Settlement Page5

15. Recitals. The Parties agree that the Recitals are incorporated into this Agreement.

16. Closure. It is the intention of the Parties in entering into this Agreement to bring closure to any and all issues between them. From the date of this Agreement forward, the Parties agree to comport themselves in a manner which is consistent with this intention.

17. Release of Attorney's Lien. In consideration of this Agreement and other good and valuable consideration (the sufficiency of which is hereby acknowledged), Kenneth Joe's counsel, Phillip Aaron, hereby waives, discharges and releases the Catholic Bishop, its present or former directors, officers, members, clergy, bishops, priests, employees, agents, attorneys, insurers, representatives, predecessors, successors and assigns, affiliates, and Rev. Victor E. Stewart, and his successors and executors, of and from any and all claims for attorney's fees, by lien or otherwise, for legal services rendered by Kenneth Joe's counsel in connection with this case. Phillip Aaron certifies that no other person is entitled to any attorney's fees in connection with the above-described matters.

The Parties have signed this Agreement effective as of the date provided above.

X _____6/9/06_____
Date

X _____[signature]_____
Kenneth Joe

_____6/20/06_____
Date

Catholic Bishop of Chicago, a corporation sole

By: _____[signature]_____

Its: _____Vicar General_____

As to Paragraph 17 (release of attorney's lien):

_____6/14/06_____
Date

_____[signature]_____
Phillip Aaron
Attorney for Kenneth Joe
Suite 200
4020 East Madison Street
Seattle, WA 98112-3150
Phone: 206-323-4466

Settlement Page 6

Scene 2

Let all bitterness, wrath, anger, clamor, and evil speaking be put away from you, with all malice.
And be kind to one another, tenderhearted, forgiving one another, just as God in Christ forgive you.

EPHESIANS 4:31-32

Where I have been, Where I am and Where we must go

The inquest you've just read about didn't just happen in a vacuum. It was the culmination of many years of often agonizing thoughts and reflections. It has indeed been a long journey…but I have survived.

Growing up with four sisters and two brothers I was the youngest boy. My childhood should have been wonderful, being part of such a large family. And it was until the sexual abuse began. It is important to know that neglect does not have to legally fit the definition of abuse to hurt, damage or impair a child emotionally. In some ways emotional abuse can be the cruelest form of all because the bruises are not visible. Then again, nothing blemishes more mentally than sexual abuse. When this pain is inflicted by those you trust, admire and want to be loved by; the abuse can even be more hurtful and confusing. When the abuser is protected by an institution that is supposed to guide and show you how to love and treat others, your life from that moment is forever changed. When the person and institution represents the good, the pure love and hope of us all—GOD—well, what do you believe in after that?

My message is that there *is* hope, life and God after the abuse. The pain of being betrayed by your Church, parents, community and everyone else who looked the other way can be so overwhelming that it leaves you in a place of loneliness and despair. There is a way to overcome the pain. This will sound crazy to some, but ultimately forgiveness is what gets you closer to the healing process.

When all is said and done, forgiveness gives you your life back. My journey has left me aware, of how deceptive and cruel people can be. Yet it has also made me sensitive to the plight of the powerless, and an active warrior in the fight to save children from all abuse, especially the experience of sexual abuse that I myself endured for much of my childhood.

I write this book now to give a voice to the hurt, discarded and failed. Hurt, discarded and failed by the Church, the parish community and parents who were blinded by the Church and its mortal leaders.

As previously discussed I was sexually abused by the pastor of my church continuously for a period of six years. My virginity and my innocence were stolen from me when a Roman Catholic Priest introduced me to anal and oral sex. These criminal activities were veiled and rationalized by his authority. What happened to me has had a lasting impact on my life. But I have refused to let it destroy me. Clinging to bitterness, of course, would have done precisely that. Forgiveness, on the other hand, brings with it an enormous sense of freedom. A victim no more! I have seized the power of forgiveness to bring peace and love more powerfully into my own life. I have forgiven my Church, my abuser, my parents and all of the adults of the parish who closed their eyes to the things they obviously had to know on some level.

My story has broad implications. Needless to say, my case was only one of many instances of clergy sexual abuse. Too many. Each case is its own tragedy, a life torn apart by the greedy manipulation of children by those who should have genuine love for them – not self-motivated lust that cares only for its needs. If we are to wipe out sexual abuse and change our future as a Church, the Roman Catholic Church must acquire the courage to admit its failures and to forgive itself. If this happens, then real change can take place. Those in the clergy who do not and have not reported abuse during their ministry must be asked to leave. This policy and this policy alone is our only hope of effecting change. It will go a long way towards restoring the confidence of the faithful in the hierarchy that has let them down so profoundly on this issue.

I have chosen to forgive my Church and claim it for my life. I have chosen to be brave and tell a story I know must be told. Can my

Church be as forgiving to itself? Can my Church brave the realities and swallow the bitter pill, which will enable it to heal and become a stronger Church? Will my Church understand that true understanding does not come from a monetary settlement! Not once did anyone in Leadership in the Archdiocese of Chicago say "I apologize for what we as a Church did to you". Acknowledgement does not come from a check. The Church must give more of itself to the healing. Is it to much to think that maybe the Cardinal of each diocese should meet with the "victim" once the settlement is reached. And if anyone thinks that it does not or shouldn't matter, think of being raped. Now think of seeing the person every Sunday, putting money in the offertory to support the rapist etc. It sounds foolish right? Well, this is an internal conflict that adult victims have to deal with. It does not have to be the actual Priest who abused them to make them feel the trauma. Every priest represents the Church and the Church in essence is the perpetrator! The Church, My Church must do more to help heal. My Church must show it's heart to these victims even more than it has shown its' check book!

Childhood

I grew up on the south side of Chicago in a housing project with my mother, four sisters and two brothers. We were poor, but we had a good support network. It was the Church. We were the only Catholic kids in the neighborhood and one of the few who went to a private school.

Having a large sib group had its benefits. Being next to the youngest, however, had its natural drawbacks. You were the youngest but not the baby, so you got ignored to a large degree. My baby sister was two years younger and had meningitis. Doctors said she would never walk. But, by the grace of God, she did recover, though she lost a good deal of her hearing and was defined as legally deaf. For as long as I could remember my mother favored my little sister. This was natural and acceptable to me. My mother also favored my older brother who was two years older than me and younger than our oldest brother by four years. This was confusing to me. I was younger, but he received all of the attention. He would later fall victim to my abuser as well.

All in all, though, life was manageable until Fr. V. entered our lives. We participated in Sunday School, youth groups, served as altar servers and got involved in just about everything else that young Catholic kids do. My mother was parish council president and always seemed to be leading something. She even worked at Catholic Charities of Chicago for 10+ years before being laid off.

Our Church was wonderful before Fr. V. The people were the Church before Fr. V. After he became Pastor, however, the Church became Fr. V. He was the first black Pastor, he was charismatic and a good leader. But the goals of his ministry were warped. He immediately began tearing down the structures that would compete for his control over the Church. The Sisters of Mercy nuns who had been with the Church for as long as I can remember as a child soon fell victim to his strength and scheme. I actually thought it was cool when I heard him yell at Sister N, who did have an attitude at times. Nonetheless, she had always been in the Parish and was part of our family. Fr. V. would soon control the Church and destroy families without a whisper from the parishioners who had grown up together and who had always protected each other before Fr. V. arrived.

My mother, who had eight children, had her favorites. My older sister, who was second oldest overall, was one of her favorites. My two sisters in the next sib-group were irrelevant to my mother. I was the second oldest in my sib-group and I was considered the oddball and treated as such by my mother. Once the abuse started with Fr. V. I struggled to feel the love from my mother although I know she loves me. Feeling unloved, coupled with her willingness to "give me up," would lead to me being delivered into the hands of a serial molester. Not knowing her actions would also lead to one of her favorites, my second oldest brother, falling victim to the abuse as well.

My biological father and my sister's father were the only men involved in my life. The older sib group's father was not around and they considered my father their father. As a child and in happier times, I felt that he was more of a father to them than to me. My older brother and sisters who were not my father's children, thought he was the greatest. Me and my full brother and sister never understood what was the great thing our older half brothers and sisters saw in my father.

After we were born, my mother and father seemed to have a love hate relationship that would affect all three of us during our lives. His selfishness as a parent contributed to his allowing the abuse to happen. As an adult I would discover that my mother never could show her love for me when all she could see was my father in me. This would hinder our relationship to this day. Her selfishness as a woman, who was hurt by this man (my father) outweighed her duty as a parent. Her love of my brother would be rooted in control and the same selfishness that damaged our relationship. In my brother she saw something she could hurt my father with. Controlling his oldest son. This would backfire on her and he would later suffer the most due to her selfishness. She would equally damage my younger sister through this same selfishness and would cause her to settle for a life of abuse by men. My mother's heart was so broken by my father that till this day their relationship remains tense. Much of this is due to my mother who can not forget the pain she feels my father caused her.

In 1996 I decided to change my last name from Nolan to Joe. I simply wanted to have my biological father's last name before I got married instead of my step-father's name. My mother was not happy about this. My sister and my brother were going to do the same thing, but my mother influenced them not to do so. On my baptismal certificate, my father is listed as Arthur Joe Nolan. Instead of putting his name as Arthur J. Joe Sr. which is his correct name, she put his name down in a way to make herself look like a good Catholic by us all having the same last name of Nolan. My father was deeply hurt by this and it negatively influenced the relationship he had with his children. My father of course disputes the pain he caused and points out the pain she caused him. After almost 30 years the scars remain fresh. Not allowing these scars to heal stood in the way of things that mattered. Ultimately they stood in the way of my father spending time with his children. One of the most important things that the children wanted was sacrificed due to my parent's adult stuff. My father will be 80 years old in 2007 and he is doing well. Having served in two wars, he has more than the emotional scars from my mother in him. I am happy to say that I and my father are very close now. Since my wedding in 1997, my father has attended the Church me and my wife got married at faithfully. He visits me in Atlanta and we enjoy having this time with each other. Even though we can not change our past, we have made great memories together over the last 10+years.

My mother went through a lot with, my oldest sister Angela who was diagnosed with mental illness in her childhood. I think the struggles with Angela drained my mother. It was as if her spirit was broken in this area. My mother could have been a better mother, yet in many ways *she was better than most*. Her biggest mistake is she believed in the Church too much. It was what she was raised to do. As many do, she was taught and believed that her belief in clergy was tied to her belief in the Church. Hopefully those who read my story receive the message that God is not a relationship with you and the Church. Your relationship with God is private and personal. A middleman is not needed. I wish this had been clear to my parents and adults who were around me during my abuse. But, of course, it wasn't.

Like many Catholic boys I grew up wanting to be a priest. I was an acolyte-altar boy, sang in the school choir, was in the youth group, went to Sunday school and participated in all the activities that good Catholic boys and girls did. In my parish it was truly a family. Every family seemed to have grown through school and Church with each other. Everyone was your mother and father. Every child felt safe, loved, supported and nurtured. Every activity in the Church seemed to be kid focused even when it was not. The kids in the parish, even the kids in the school who didn't come to church regularly, were part of our family and we felt safe around each other.

There were always two other boys and I who hung around the church all the time. However, we were always chased out of the rectory by the long-time house-keeper, Ms. B. As I shared previously, she was a stern little woman who ran the rectory like her private military camp. She lived in the rectory and it was literally her home.

From Abused to Protector

As a kid I did not like her much, as an adult I began to appreciate her for boundaries and consistency. The one time I and the boys walked around the rectory we went into the then pastor's suite and saw that he had cable on the TV. We were surprised to discover that he had the sex channel subscription. When we turned it on and saw it we quickly turned it off and ran out of the room. I don't think we ever talked about it after that day. This pastor was new to us, but he had been a priest in the parish forever. And he was a good priest to us. The sex channel was shocking to stumble upon, but we didn't care and it had no lasting impression. My years in the parish following this period couldn't be more different. I like to think that my childhood consisted of two periods "before and after Fr. V.".

Moreover, my father did not consistently spend quality time with us. My mother, I think, was happy to have a male role model for me. The fact that he was a priest was a huge plus, I believe, to my mom. Fr. V. began to buy me things that my mother could never afford. My behavior began to spiral out of control. I was always challenging, but not like this. I could not stand to see my mother, as every day she was content with me being with him. As the abuse increased to anal sex my behavior became more defiant.

As I became more and more detached from my mother an incident at school changed everything. Ms. A., who was a teacher's aide at the school and as sweet as pie, thought I cursed at her. I did not, but she called my mother and told her I did. I knew I would get a whipping and I knew my mom would not listen to me. I went home and hid under clothes in my sister's room. I wanted to run away, but I chickened out. When my mother came home they searched for me for at least an hour. One of my sisters found me and my mother whipped me; she wouldn't listen to my side of the story.

I became even more bitter towards her. She told my father, who told me on the phone he would be coming to see me. When he came over he took me up to my sister's room asked me what happened and I told him I didn't do it. He told me to take off my clothes and then he whipped me. This incident shut my heart and soul off to my father until I graduated from college. Soon I had shut myself off to my whole family. I was hurting so bad inside. My attitude towards my mother was cold and blunt.

In anger one day my mother yelled at me and said, "I am tired of you, if someone else can deal with you fine, go." My heart broke. Although I was not responding to her it was not what I wanted. I called the only person who wanted me: Fr. V. He picked me up. I only returned home after that day to pick up my clothes and to visit occasionally.

Shortly after the abuse started Fr. V. took me on a trip to Six Flags Great America in Gurnee, Illinois. This was a big deal to me as I believe it was only my second time going. Such a trip would have been too costly for my mother. Again, having eight children meant that we were loved, we had what we needed, however there was little room in the budget for us to have what we wanted. My abuse for the next six years would afford me all of the niceties which as I know now was the systematic manipulation to keep me focused on those things and not on the abuse being done to me. Trips to Great America would become regular. Early in the abuse we would go on one of the biggest trips he would take me on. We went to Rome Italy! Now what we know now this would raise suspicion of why kids would be traveling with a grown man outside of a school field trip or like activity. We got passports and just went on a trip. My brother, two older boys and 1 of the Church Deacons also went. No one asked questions on the trip when I was alone in his room with him or when we just disappeared. As hard as it is to believe, Fr. V. molested me several times while we were in Rome, minutes away from the Vatican. Although this was to be a holy trip for Fr., his lust could not even be subsided in this, spiritual trip that he held close to his heart. He was moved as we visited the catacombs and as we walked up the stairs to the top of the Vatican. He would often times go to himself and read his bible when we were out in the court yard of the Vatican and other holy places. After the trip to Rome we would routinely have places that we visited yearly. Every other year or so we drove to Canada. These trips were always fun. Usually there would be 3-4 other boys with us so I would not have to worry about being molested everyday during the trip. Fr.

V.'s appetite as mentioned previously was insatiable. When we visited Canada we stayed in Toronto most of the time. I remember thinking how could we be so close to another country when you could just walk over the bridge and be in Buffalo, NY. Of course I know better now, but it was fascinating to find other whole countries were that close to us. When we visited Québec we soon discovered it was not the vacationing destination for us! Honestly, the people were rude and they all spoke French. Maybe the rudeness came from the fact we did not speak French and they could not understand us. We however visited Québec on each trip we made to Canada because we loved the Hotel that we stayed at each visit. The hotel was wonderful and the people that ran the hotel were extremely kind. During one of the trips when I was in high school, I managed to sneak and have a flirtatious relationship with a girl on vacation in Toronto. I don't remember her name, but I remember sneaking out to meet her anytime I knew Fr. V. was occupied. When one of the other boys was in his room alone with him, I pretty much knew I had several hours that I would not be on his radar. One place that we visited at least two times a year was the Trappist Monastery of Our Lady of New Mallery right outside of Dubuque, Iowa. Prior to coming to St. Charles Lwanga, Fr. V. lived at the Monastery for over a year debating whether he was called to that life. He obviously decided that living as a monk was not his calling, however this is the one place where I think his lustful craving for boys was somehow curtailed by his true desire for spiritual enlightness. This was the one place where I felt truly safe from his appetite. There was a monk named Bro. Jarrod who Fr. V. was close to and who was a free spirit. He would sneak out at night and go bowling with us. He was a lot of fun and he was a sincere holy gentle giant. Br. Jarrod stood about 7 ft tall, however his spiritual presence was evident upon meeting him. Br. Jarrod would have a series of heart attacks and would eventually succumb during my high school years from his ongoing heart problems.

    When we went on these trips Fr. V. usually always brought other boys along except in the beginning of my abuse when I was the sole focus. However, there were some activities such as retreats and other speaking engagements that I would attend with Fr. V. alone. Because of this I was very versed in spiritual works of Sister Teresa of Avila and St. John of the Cross. From the castles of Sister Teresa to the true deep spiritual teachings of John of the Cross, I was well versed and I sincerely felt close to God. Many would say how is that when I was enduring sexual abuse for such a long period of time? Well I never felt God abandoned me. Never, not even a little bit. I believe my heart was protected by God. I could have become bitter and angry against the world. Instead I became vigilante, absolute and totally connected to the hurt of others. I don't have a save the world attitude, I am to much of a realist for that. However, I have dedicated my life to ensuring children are not abused and the voiceless particularly poor families are not trampled on by the powers that be. Poverty breeds risk. What comes first the bad decisions of the parents or the pressing world that poverty stricken families often feel crushed by. My abuse has led me to not see the world so black and white. My mother in some parts of the country would have had all of her children removed from her care once the abuse was disclosed? Sometimes Child Welfare is administered as though we have to "blame" someone for the abuse happening. Some would say she did not do enough to protect me. In reality society did not do enough to protect me. There are no such thing as secrets when you evaluate the victims that are still coming forward disclosing the abuse at the hands of their priest. People knew, so it wasn't a secret. Well again some will read this and say of course it is clear that bishops, priest and other church officials knew and covered it up. The bishops, the priest and other clergy ultimately report to the people! My mother's eyes were closed as much as society's eyes were closed at the possibility that priest could actually take advantage of their trusted status given to them by society. Many people will read this and say, "I would have never let this or that happen. I would have made better decisions for my child". Really? What latitude do you give clergy now with children? This type of abuse will continue in the church until "we" as a church demand that our church do the right thing concerning the protection and care of our children. Every parish should have open scheduled dialogue to talk about the do's and don'ts as related to anyone in the church caring for children on activities or working with children regularly in church groups. Some communities will say, "we don't have that problem". There is no use of addressing the issue when it has not affected us". That unfortunately is part of the problem that led to the years of "systematic secrecy" within the church. How do you know you have not been affected? I bet most parishes that have had to deal with this hurt as a congregation thought the same thing until their priest who they have grown up with and children have been baptized by was found to have sexually molested/raped children. This is a call to everyone to wake up and expect the same standards we expect from teachers, doctors, lawyers, social workers and all who operate with a trust that must be given by the community. I say trust with supervision. We must end the blind trust that we have given to the church. Even now our church struggles with focusing on the right response versus the liability of giving the right response. If we care about children as I know we do as a people built on faith, we must ask and demand an understanding of how we want our children to be treated and cared for in our parishes. We must be preventive and proactive by talking as a faith community of how we will enforce standards that protect our children. We do not need directives from the bishop's or the Pope in order to decide what should be done in our parishes. Should those in ministries working with children undergo background checks? Should their always be two adults when working with children? These are only some questions that could be asked and decided by faith communities. For those that say this is over the top, I hope the necessity for proactiveness is not triggered by someone you love being victim to this abuse. I say we must all "care enough" to be involved in this solution. We can all agree that our children deserve no less.

Where I have been, Where I am and Where we must go

Fr. Stewart praying while we are in Rome.

Fr. Stewart & his mother 1986 Mother's Day before she died in 1987. Fr. preaching at St. Charles Lwanga.

Scene 3

Let the beauty of the Lord our God be upon us, and establish the work of our hands for us; yes, establish the work of our hands.

PSALM 90:17

Life After the Abuse

After college I was prepared to go to law school. During my college years I maintained a full-time job in order to gain some independence and move away from the control of Fr. V. He made it clear when I went to college that he did not want me to work. When he found out I was working he was upset, but he had to accept it. I worked many jobs in social work and child welfare. I worked with troubled youth, Developmentally Delayed/Mentally Ill (DD/MI) and elderly populations.

From these various jobs I had duties that ranged from sponge baths to mentoring. And everything else in-between! I learned a lot of humility and a lot of appreciation for life on these jobs. For example, working with grown men who were so disfigured with cerebral palsy that from afar you may think they were also mentally challenged. I learned that my stereotypes were in fact baseless and small. These men were happy with life even though their bodies were uncontrollable, spastic, etc. It's funny, but it became a privilege for me to work for them in their homes. When the little uncomfortable moments come in life I attempt to take myself back to their faces. Back to their acceptance of life, no matter how physically uncomfortable it is.

Then there were the elderly who I worked with in the nursing home. It was heartbreaking to see Alzheimer's take proud men and women and steal everything in their minds from them without them knowing. To see the families cry when their loved ones did not remember them was very difficult. However, to hear them tell the stories of the lives of their mothers, fathers, sisters and brothers who couldn't remember them was like playing a video. It was wonderful and I felt honored to hear the stories and appreciated the opportunity to get to know the person who couldn't tell me their own story.

I realized that mental illness was truly a disease when working with MI men in their homes. At times they could be the most helpful, lovable person. Next minute they are physically attacking you. I learned that I did not want to work with this population.

Working at Job Corps with youth was the most rewarding. I realized that I could give them something I did not have, a male role model that was positive and interested in helping them the right way. I found out many had their own abusive situations that they were attempting to handle. I wanted to not judge, but be as helpful as I could to offer support and direction for help. I knew that I did not want any of them to ever hurt the way that I did. Many of the girls were promiscuous because they had been mistreated by older boys or men. Many of the boys were in trouble due to not knowing their fathers or having to hustle or were messed up on drugs. Many were simply following their parents' lead. I remember encouraging them to complete their GED at Job Corps and to take advantage of the trades that were taught there. This was done in-between playing cards with them, lifting them back up when their fragile family relationships let them down, when they broke curfew and came back drunk, etc. It was through this experience that I learned to never give up on a child. I was deeply touched by all of my experiences, but I was personally affected by the youth in a way unlike any of my other experiences; after all, I saw myself in their eyes. Even though I knew this, I still was not aware of my true calling.

Upon graduation from college, I was sure I was going to be a lawyer. I remember being concerned about the expense of law school. I had applied and got accepted to an internship in the office of then late Senator Paul Simon of Illinois. During these years Fr. V. had already had brain surgery, recovered and was away from children. The diocese had him tucked away in a nursing facility as a chaplain. I would still go and see him; his memory was bad and his predatory instincts were, I think, almost gone. One of my fraternity brothers was the Interim Executive Director/President of the agency he had worked at for years. When he described the work his agency performed, I was immediately interested. It involved working with children in foster care. I figured this could be my stop until I figured out what I would do regarding law school.

Well, I never looked back. My first job was working with intact families. I worked with families that needed help in order to prevent the possible placement of the children in foster care. To this day, the families I worked with are fresh in my mind. These families were my family, your family, they were regular families. They could be your family member, neighbor, church member or boss. They were families who had run in to hard times and were trying to get through it. I was hooked.

Over the next 15 years I would work various jobs in Child Welfare, from caseworker to Executive Director of Agencies. Some of the most rewarding but challenging work was when I worked in group homes and residential treatment centers. In these environments you work closely with the kids, almost living with them. I was privileged to have seen lives changed, though sadly I saw more lost. During these years I obtained both of my Masters' degrees while working fulltime. My drive in these years was to get into higher leadership positions where I could affect policy and actions of staff as it related to children and families involved in foster care. As a worker I tried to make a difference. I wanted to help families reunite in a system that did not always welcome it. As a direct line supervisor, I tried to train workers to know that going that extra mile was necessary in our business. I wanted them to always know that in our field, the right heart was more important than completing the right form.

For a long time my dream job was front line supervisor. I wanted so much to teach workers how to do the work the right way when working with children and families in Child Welfare. As a worker I had seen families hurt by what workers *did not do*. I wanted to train workers how to serve and never compromised on this. Training people at the various agencies where I supervised workers was one of my greatest gifts to the field of Child Welfare.

Paradoxically, however the *greatest* gift ever given to me was the sexual abuse that I endured by Fr. V. This sounds crazy I know. I am not saying I was lucky or glad that I was abused! Absolutely not!

However, I am sure at this point in my life I would not be who I am and I would not be the Child Welfare professional that I am if I had not been down the road of abuse myself. For 15 years of my professional career, I chose to not deal with my scars. Even after Fr. V. died I chose to continue my life and not deal with the pain and hurt that I had endured. I chose to use my hurt to drive me to make the right decisions for children and families. I only finally chose to come forward when my brother asked me to. I chose to support him and to own my own story.

Having left Illinois and moved to Georgia for new work challenges, I never thought I would be thrust into the middle of a lawsuit with the Archdiocese of Chicago. Over the years many had already sued the diocese for abuse they had suffered at the hands of Fr. V. I had heard of the settlements and the things that were said. This was happening while I was in Illinois. I knew that some of the things that people were saying were exaggerated and untrue. However, I refused to speak. The abuse they suffered was real and regardless of exaggeration, their pain was real.

When I decided to support my brother, I demanded one thing of the lawyer who had represented many of the boys, who are now men, in previous suits against the diocese concerning Fr. V. Do not attach my story or my name to anyone. My story is my own. My pain is my own and how I use it is my choice alone. I chose not to be used. I was not bitter against Fr. V., I had forgiven him years ago. I had to, otherwise I would have destroyed myself. Even when I was holding it together during the 15 years before I pursued acknowledgment from the Diocese of Chicago, I was self destructing with alcohol. It could have gone either way for me. I truly believe God had a plan for me.

Moving on through Forgiveness

I have forgiven my abuser, my Church, my parish community, my parents and mostly myself for the abuse I endured. Over the years it has been most difficult to forgive myself. It may sound silly, but for many years I felt I should have been stronger, in order to prevent the abuse. Not so much the abuse I suffered, but the abuse of the 40 – 50 other young boys who were victimized during the years of my abuse. Father's appetite was like a bottomless pit. He did not seem to have a specific age, body type, etc. He wanted all the boys he came in contact with. I have often thought in my adult years, if I had been strong enough to tell someone, than maybe the numerous other boys wouldn't have been abused. Thinking rationally, I know that it is not my fault that I or anyone else was abused. However, a part of me feels guilty and responsible for not standing up and making it known what was going on through those years. My guilt mixed with my pain, caused me to abuse alcohol, be sexually promiscuous and to be overly suspicious about adults around children. I have moved to a better place with these things with the love of my wife and the joy of my son. My decision to come forward and tell my story to the Archdiocese had a lot to do with giving validation to the stories that I knew so many of those boys (now men) were telling and to free my soul from the mental prison that this type of abuse puts you in. I knew that the only way I could say that I truly was not letting this episode in my life control me, was by facing the story and I could only do that by telling the story. I wanted to stand up now for those who were victims of Fr. V. that were struggling with life because of how the abuse affected them.

People cope differently with abuse. Some use it as a motivating entity to overcome. Many, unfortunately, get lost in the pain and become self-destructive. Drugs, abuse towards others and sexual identity issues are only a couple of the many ways sexual abuse attempts to conquer the soul. My coping in regards to my abuse led me to defiant behavior and a *me against the world* type of attitude. These behaviors served me very well; however, there were plenty of times that this attitude cost me a great deal. Bar fights, drunken behavior and damage to close relationships. By the grace of God, my misdemeanors never cost me things that were permanently fractured or otherwise, damaged.

My career in Child Welfare has been a therapeutic outlet for me to feel empowered to help prevent children from enduring the pain of abuse. I have now been working in Foster Care/Child Welfare for 17 years. My first job after college was as a caseworker for intact families. The families I worked with had difficulties that if left unchecked, could lead to the children coming in to care. The families, as I mentioned earlier, were no different than my family or yours. The issues that the families faced were exaggerated due to being poor. I am so glad that I started my Foster Care/Child Welfare career with intact families, because it gave me an inside view to the needs of families and why it was so important to help families stay together if they safely could. Although some of the parents may have struggled with decision-making in parenting, and didn't make the best choices to improve their situation; there was one thing they did get right; they loved their children. This first job gave me an insight that I have always attempted to keep in mind when I am making decisions concerning children and families: It could be you, so remember to not judge and treat them with the dignity and respect that you would expect.

This philosophy is part of my passion for helping children. I attempt to listen to the child in a way denied me. Listening to children is not always through words. When listening we have to listen for the heart. We have to feel the spirit coming out of the body. We need to watch what the face, arms and the rest of the body tells us. We have to want to hear the child in order to receive their message. If the adults around me had only listened they would have heard. They would have heard me yelling. Heard me crying. Heard me wanting to be saved. Every situation in which I have to make a decision or give input on a child/family, I try to listen. I try to hear the words not being said. As I reflect on my own abuse, it could have been prevented if the adults would have listened. If they would not have ignored the obvious signs. If they did not look at Fr. V. as a "god" instead of an imperfect man. The freedom that he was allowed to have with me and other children in the parish would never be allowed by a parent if it was someone else. For example, a parent wouldn't allow their child to visit with a grown man in his bedroom! This happened frequently without question. To some degree this type of behavior is what made me go back to school to obtain my two M.S. degrees.

In my career I have worked with a lot of Child Welfare professionals who have taught me how to do the right work, what spirit you need to do the right work and why we must always be serious about the work we do. One of my old supervisors once told me, "We have to work to get it right all the time because even when we do the best work we can do, bad things will still happen to children. So when we don't do our best work we have increased those odds more."

In my career I have worked with more people who have worked with the "Right Heart" than I have not. However, I have worked with a good number of Child Welfare professionals who treat children and families according to policy…and nothing else. Now don't get me wrong, we need policy to do our work; however the implementation of policy is only administered correctly if the "Right Heart" is guiding the implementation. This type of work is what inspired me to go back and get my advanced degrees. I wanted so much to ensure that workers who worked with children and families involved with foster care or other aspects of Child Welfare were being taught to implement policy with the "Right Heart".

When I began my career in Child Welfare I saw many workers and supervisors hide behind policy because they were mistreating natural parents or foster parents. As I tell folks when I do trainings or have a platform; no policy in Child Welfare has ever been written to oppress, disrespect or demean. It is the spirit in which policies are implemented that causes negative feelings of abandonment and hopelessness. I have struggled in my career to have patience with those who I feel do not have the right spirit/heart in serving. It is a privilege for us to serve children and families. However, at times I believe that we treat children and families as if we are doing them a favor. My abuse has made me sensitive and passionate to those in need. It has made me intolerably impatient with professionals in our field who make decisions regarding children who are hurting with bureaucratic thinking and political agendas. It is heartbreaking and should be criminal when we make decisions that are not solely based on the best interest of the children. It should be clear when I say the best interest of the children I naturally include the family in the equation. Children are attached to families; if we ignore the family we are ignoring the child. The two are not separate entities in separate worlds. Many supervisors fail in their instructions to caseworkers by stating policy only and not talking about how policy may affect the child and the family. My heart has been overwhelmed by the last 17 years I have worked in the field. I have relived the same closed eyes, turned heads and passive perceptions in Child Welfare professionals that led to my abuse by Fr. V. in my parish. It is this behavior that leads to abuse in many situations.

Adults must not close their eyes or give the benefit of the doubt when their "right" mind tells them something is not right. Children depend on this from adults in order to ensure they are safe. When adults fail to act children get hurt, emotionally, physically or both. I have forgiven the adults who failed me. I have forgiven my Church and my abuser. I claim now, however, as an adult to fight for children in an effort to prevent hurt. I am not as forgiving to adults who work in the field who do not work with the seriousness of mind and heart to minimize pain and hurt when they can.

I am not so forgiving to our state and federal governments who choose to spend more money on road projects than on the protection of our children and the strengthening of our families. I am not so forgiving in our continued failure to do all that we can to protect children in this world. Having been sexually abused for years, I know the pain of feeling let down and wanting to be saved by the adults around you. It is a pain that stays with you in your mind. Long after the body has healed the mind and the heart lives on in a life long healing process. In no way am I indicating that the field of Child Welfare has acted in the obvious intentional irresponsible way that the Roman Catholic Church (and other churches) did. Yet there are still problems to be solved, and much work to be done.

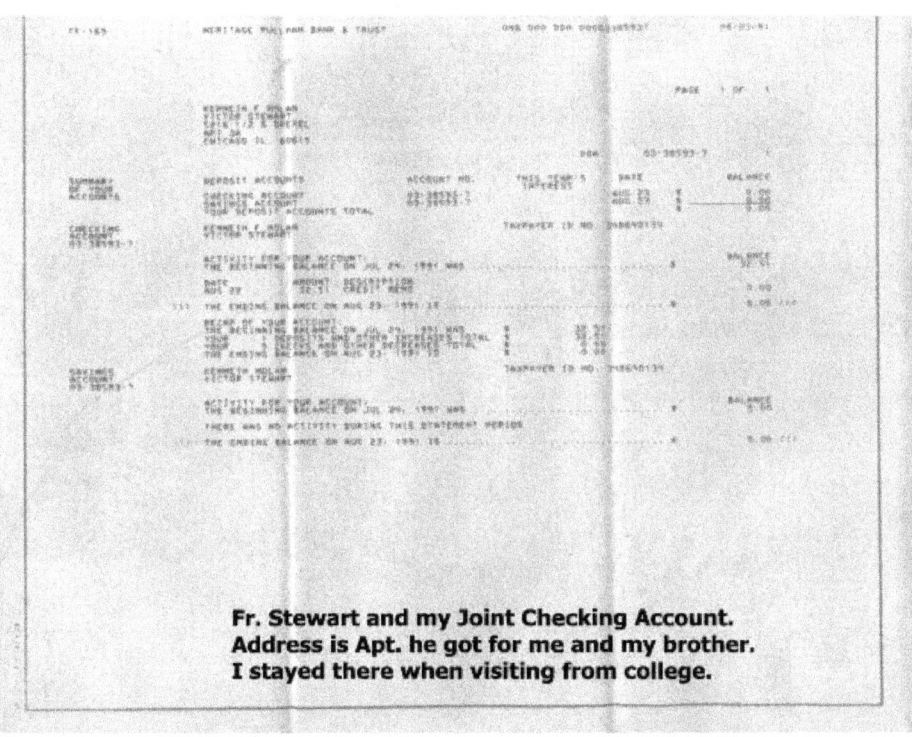

**Fr. Stewart and my Joint Checking Account.
Address is Apt. he got for me and my brother.
I stayed there when visiting from college.**

From Abused to Protector

High School Graduation and Bday, 5/24/1987. Mom did not attend, Fr. Stewart taking pictures. Abuse diminished greatly at this time.

Life After the Abuse

Prom 1987 in Rectory Kitchen. Fr. Stewart took pictures.

Scene 4

Love your enemies, bless those who curse you, do good to those who hate you, and pray for those who spitefully use you and persecute you, that you may be sons of your Father in heaven.

MATTHEW 5:44-45

Thoughts and Reflections

It is far too easy to listen to a story such as mine and confine all of our criticism for the Church. Yet that would be terribly shortsighted. Clearly, the problem of child abuse is widespread throughout our society, and it needs to be addressed at all levels. What lessons can we learn from the entire debacle involving the Church?

A good place to start is by recognizing where to place the blame. The leadership? Yes…but only in part. While there are no excuses – none – for the blind eye that those in positions of Church leadership exhibited for decades, that does not mean that they are the only ones culpable. True, they did indeed fail in their duties and responsibilities, and the outrage expressed by the laity is quite understandable. However, the failure did not begin and it does not end simply amongst the hierarchy. The adults of the various Parish communities allowed this cycle of denial to be perpetuated. Their silence and lack of action led to the continued suffering of so many children. We must adapt a new mind-set, a way of thinking that puts children's safety first. Worrying about the "embarrassment" of a scandal should never stand between reporting and / or preventing a horrific crime.

Some people think that the secretive, insular, self-protective nature of the Church makes its failings unique. They believe that similar problems would not happen with the State. Unfortunately, the various levels of government have their own problems when it comes to dealing with child abuse. Far too often, the Child Welfare / Foster care profession is tarnished by the intrusion of politics. The cycle works like this: a politician runs on a platform of protecting children. It sounds good and he/she gets elected. But then if the people are dissatisfied with the politician's efforts, he/she is booted out of office and the cycle begins all over again with a new candidate.

I consider the politicization of this issue a national disgrace. Children's lives are not some political football to be thrown around by those whose only real agenda is gaining power. All of us as a society need to let go of the political aspect of this problem and, instead, treat it as the very basic *human* problem that it truly is. We need to collectively ask ourselves as a people, do we really love and care enough for our children –ALL of them – to do whatever is necessary to ensure their safety? If the answer is anything other than a resounding Yes, we as a society are failing every bit as much as the Church has failed on this critical issue.

As with the Church, when it comes to the State it's far too easy to place the blame solely on those in positions of authority such as elected officials, judges, Caseworkers, Casework Supervisors, etc. However, do we take the time and effort to be active neighbors and responsible adults? Do we care if other children are treated as well as we treat our own children?

Let me put this in more concrete terms. If you see children getting into a dangerous situation, playing on railroad tracks, for example, do you simply look the other way? Be honest. If so, why? Do you think, *it's not my child...let his parents worry about it?* That kind of mentality is far too common in our society today, in large part because we've lost a sense of genuine community and fellowship in which people actually care for one another, and the safety of children is seen as every adult's obligation and duty.

Sometimes the situations we find ourselves in are not so clear-cut. It may simply be that we see an adult interacting with a child in a way that makes us uncomfortable and maybe a bit suspicious. The natural inclination is to just turn our heads and look the other way. But that is not fair to the child who may be in jeopardy! Remember that famous case in New York City many years ago where a woman was brutally attacked and her neighbors, who heard her screams, didn't even bother to pick up the phone and dial 911. That was an indicator of how crass people have become to the plight of their neighbors…yet who is more vulnerable than our children?

I think part of the problem is that people – good people at heart – feel that the problems of child abuse in this country are just too big for them to do anything about it. The problems are overwhelming, so what can any one individual do to make a difference? The fact of the matter is, there is plenty that all of us can do. One small step is to address the political conundrum I mentioned earlier. Be an active participant in the electoral process and don't let any of the politicians from any political party play a cynical game with our children's well being. Demand excellence from Child Welfare agencies both public and private. It's a travesty that many Child Welfare agencies allow low-performing staffers to stay on the job simply because of the fear of turnover. In other words, there will be no continuity if a different caseworker is brought onto a case. That's true, but if a worker is not visiting a child in foster care at least monthly, then how can safety be evaluated? The system can indeed be very short-sighted sometimes, which is why it's all the more important for every adult in our society to play an active role when it comes to our children's safety. How well we do says a lot about who we are as a people.

In my own case, what happened to me as a child molded who I am as an adult, and today I am a Child Welfare professional. For me, none of this is "theoretical" or stuff you learn out of a book. I've lived through abuse, so I can relate to these kids and their families in a special way, with insights that others may well overlook. I know, for example, that for any agency that deals with children to be successful, it's an absolute must that they have leaders with strong skills and lots of guts. Why do I say guts? Because true leadership means making tough decisions, including dismissing any staff members who talk down to those whom they are supposed to be serving. Furthermore, supervisors who allow workers to not return calls or miss scheduled appointments with families without calling in advance must be held accountable. If they do not change and improve their behavior, they should no longer be working for the agency.

Do things like this really happen amongst, Child Welfare professionals? Sadly, the answer is yes. Please don't misunderstand. There are legions of dedicated, caring people who have chosen this field as their career and do excellent work. However, there are also many others who are just there for the paycheck and who feel it's perfectly OK to "lay down on the job." Well, I've developed quite a reputation, in Illinois and especially in Georgia, for never tolerating such an approach when it comes to the safety and welfare of children. The kids and their families deserve better than that from the very people who are obliged by law and by simple human decency to support them! You might be surprised by how many children in foster care never even receive a happy birthday card from their caseworker. How much caring does that show these children? More to the point, how would you feel if it was *your* child?

If what I'm saying sounds like I'm being harsh on those who shirk their duties and responsibilities when it comes to helping children, maybe I am. Yet I make no apologies, because I have such an outlook for a very good reason: I am extremely sensitive to the needs of those who have no voice, both children and adults. These are people for whom it is far too easy for "the system" to simply overlook and sweep under the bureaucratic rug. It is alarmingly similar to the way the Church handled matters of child molestation, allowing authority figures (such as Father V.) to abuse their power and position to intimidate the powerless into silence. I am determined not to let that happen within any of the agencies that I work for. I think the business we are in is far too serious—and the consequences of incompetence too severe—to ever adapt an attitude of complacency or an acceptance of mediocrity in performance.

Having worked in this field for many years (I was Director of two of Georgia's biggest Public Sector Child Welfare Programs) I have seen firsthand the problems facing our children. And one phenomenon that I have seen far too often is the tendency that people have to become judgmental when it comes to families where children need to be removed. Yes, the child's safety (i.e., preventing further abuse) must always come first. However, we need to treat every family with dignity and respect throughout the entire process. Think about it. Other children may well come into that family in the future, so we must be prepared to help them in any way that we can so that no other child who will live in that home will have to suffer abuse.

Not only must we be less judgmental, especially when it comes to issues such as corporal punishment, we must make sure that our focus (both as a society in general and child advocacy agencies in particular) continues to be on the prevention of abuse.

We have to get better at recognizing just what exactly constitutes "neglect," too. It can't be allowed to be diluted into a one-size-fits-all term that covers every potential situation, from a dirty house to a child who may not be receiving adequate medical attention. One thing, however, I am certain of: being poor should not equal neglect! Anytime we bring a child into foster care when we should instead be assisting the family that in itself is abusive. And it happens far too often. Is our goal really to "strengthen families," as the politicians like to say? It should be, but, tragically, in many cases we've foolishly turned it into a matter of children vs. parents, with the State on the side of the child. That misses half of the equation. We want to help the children precisely by helping the families to help themselves. So often this very basic concept is completely misunderstood.

The problem of child abuse (both physical and sexual) is a homegrown terrorist threat right under our noses. But we are not powerless to fight against this pernicious threat. It's a complex topic, but here is a summation of things average people can do to make children's lives better:

1. Parents need to be watchful of all children as if they were their own.
2. Parents should know the parents and other family members of their children's friends before allowing them to play unsupervised or spend a night at the friend's house.
3. All parents should be involved in the PTA at school.
4. We must demand that Child Welfare programs be fully funded so that case loads are manageable.
5. Our Child Welfare system should be preventive rather than reactive. We shouldn't be working with a foster care system that doesn't graduate children and bounces them around to strangers instead of family members.

6. Churches need to require background checks for all personnel.
7. There should be a strict curfew for all children.
8. We must demand that all Child Welfare professionals be competent – especially the leaders!
9. We have to make sure that those engaged in social work have their heart in the right place. Just having the right degrees is never enough. These are jobs that require passion and commitment. There is no room for complacency.
10. Realize that, regardless of how much money we might spend, ultimately it is not up to the government to fix this problem. Communities must live up to their own responsibilities right in their own neighborhoods, schools, churches and homes. Sexual and physical abusers are no match for dogged vigilance. They can and must be stopped!

It would be impossible for me to end this discussion without reflecting on how my own childhood encounter with sexual abuse has impacted my views as an adult. Though I have now evolved to the point where I am able to forgive, that does not mean that I have forgotten what happened to me. No, it's not something that I sit around dwelling on day in and day out, yet it is part of my past and nothing can change that. I think this is the same for all people who have been abused as children. For me, I know that I was not able to reconcile myself with what had happened to me for many years. When I was still a teenager I was able to take myself to a "different place inside of me" as it were, to escape from the reality of being abused.

Of course, that only works for so long. There always comes a day of reckoning when you have to be truthful with yourself regarding what has happened in your own life. When that time for me finally came, as an adult, the feelings I had so carefully sheltered deep within myself from childhood all burst to the surface. At first, I expressed it in a sense of hatred for my Church and all the clergy (especially Father

V.) and also all of the parishioners who closed their eyes and let this happen to me. The more I thought about it, the more outraged I became. I realized that all of those years that were stolen from me could have been avoided. That's right, what happened to me did not have to happen to me! If someone had had the courage to not look the other way, all of that pain and suffering (for me and who knows how many others) could have been prevented. Just think how outraged you would feel if you came to such a realization in your own life. Not a pretty picture, is it?

To add fuel to the fire, I felt in some ways cheated that Father V. was dead. That meant that (at least in human terms) he would never have to answer for what he had done to me and the other victims. It seemed like there was no justice. He got away with it for all of those years and now I had to live with it for the rest of my life…which in many ways is the most excruciating aspect of the whole ordeal. If I had not moved from this place I would never been able to really heal. I had difficult periods. When a young man acknowledges that he has been sexually abused, an unimaginable psychological dilemma inevitably ensues. You feel conflicted. Because of the crime that had been perpetrated against you, it's unavoidable to start asking yourself if that means you are homosexual. I really did not think I was, but it did make me concerned about what others would think of me, even as an adult. Would they think I was less of a man? What would my wife think of me? My children would one day read my story—what kind of thoughts would all of this stir up in their minds about their father? It's a horrible burden to have to bear, yet you have no choice about it once you decide to go public with the truth.

Not only does this cause all of the above problems-and more-as an adult, when you are a young person going through or just emerging from sexual abuse, it has an especially negative impact on your life. For example, I recall that I had intimate encounters with boys whom I knew were also being abused by Fr. V. This involved inappropriate touching, acting out what our common molester had taught to us. Seeing these men as adults, we silently know one another's pain. I know they have been scarred by it as much as I have.

Also during my early years, I began having sex with girls at a young age. This kind of acting out, I'm sure, was part of my effort to reassure myself that I was indeed a normal, heterosexual boy. And because I am heterosexual, I desperately did not want anybody to find out about the "dirty little secret" in my life and therefore jump to wrong conclusions about me and the kind of person that I am. Let me add that this fear of exposure plays right into the hands of those in the Church who knew what was happening yet did all that they could to cover it up. They used shame and false guilt as weapons against those of us whom had been victimized, and that is one of the reasons this horrendous scandal was able to continue unabated for such an unthinkable stretch of years.

Well, now it is decades later and I am a grown man with my own family. So where has my past now led me? To further rage? To more hatred? While such feelings may seem justified, the truth is, that is not the path I've chosen to take. To the contrary, it has spurred me into action. I can't sit on the sidelines and watch, hoping that we get it right. This is especially important as I pursue my work in Child Welfare, not to mention how I live my daily life and raise my own child. I know that the family is not always to blame, and I recognize how vital it is for us to try to help families as much as possible, and be sensitive to their particular circumstances.

Lastly, having been through what happened to me as a child, I have made a firm decision not to live my life thinking of myself as a victim. And I don't want others who have been abused to think of themselves that way either. That would only give more power to their abusers. A much better, more productive response is to own your abuse, forgive your abuser and speak about it. Loudly!

Now, many of you may have been struck by something I just said...*forgive* your abuser? Yes, absolutely. In fact, I have done so myself and I am that much stronger because of it. You see, it has nothing to do with whether the abuser asked for or deserves our forgiveness, because, in the final analysis, forgiveness is not really so much about the abuser. It is about our selves. It allows us to move beyond what has happened to us and concentrate on living our own lives as best we can. Forgiveness opens up a world of opportunities for us to help others as they learn from our experience.

If I went about the world bitter because of what happened to me as a child, people would think that the experience had destroyed me. They might have pity for me, but they would not have respect. They would not think that I was somebody from whom they could learn something. But when those I come into contact with see that I am comfortable with the concept of forgiveness, and that I live as a man with confidence and faith in God and in myself—and not as a victim—then and only then are they able to hear my story and to learn valuable lessons from it. And hopefully make the world a better place to live, especially for our children

Thoughts and Reflections

Lisa, Ken Sr & Ken Jr., Easter 2006.
St. Albans, Augusta, Ga.

From Abused to Protector

Lisa, Ken Sr. & Ken Jr., Easter 2007 after Mass, Our Lady of Lourdes Church, Atlanta, GA

Ken Jr Baptisim 2001, Holy Name of Mary Church, Chicago, Il.

Thoughts and Reflections

From Abused to Protector

Scene 5

*When the whirlwind passes by, the wicked is no more,
but the righteous has an everlasting foundation.*

PROVERBS 10:25

Closure

When Fr. V. first got sick I rushed to his side. It is important to know that Fr. V. first became sick when victims first started to come out and talk about their sexual abuse at the hands of Fr. V. Fr. V. had a blood clot in his brain and had to have surgery. He lost some of his long term memory and thus would never be the same. After his surgery he went to a rehabilitative center at Rush Presbyterian St. Lukes Hospital were he lived in an apartment and was being taught how to do everyday functions to care for himself. I would often go visit him with my girlfriend at the time. I would bring him food that I knew he liked and sit and talk to him about things in the past in order to try and get his memory sharp again. This was the first time that I brought a girl around that did not bring consequences to me. He was a different man. He was a shell of who he was. It is important to remember as I talked about earlier, Fr. V. was a very intelligent man. He attended Holy Cross Elementary School and graduated from St. Ignatius High School which is one of the best in Chicago. He received a BA in Theology from Loyola University and received a STB and M. DIV degrees from the Pontifical University of St. Mary of the Lake. He was accepted into the Doctor of Ministry Program at the University of St. Mary of the Lake, however did not complete the program. It was sad for me to see this man who on one hand was the monster that abused me and took my childhood innocence and on the other hand was my parent/father/mentor who was the strongest man I had ever met. I felt I needed to protect him. I never judged or faulted the guys for coming forward when he was sick, it was never a wrong time to deal with their hurt as far as I was concerned. However, I felt it was my job to ensure that he was not alone and didn't feel that all had turned their back on him. After the surgery there was no more money, no more ability to manipulate people through material things. There were only a couple of the guys still coming around after Fr. V. had brain surgery. I can honestly say that after Fr. V. had surgery, I felt a sense of freedom. Even though part of me loved Fr. V. for caring for me and being a father to me, there was a big part that knew not to cross him. I was afraid of Fr. V. as my abuser. I saw him as the most powerful person in the world. He was invincible to me. I for the first time felt I could be my own person around him without thinking about how he may react. I knew he needed me now so he would just have to accept me bringing girls around. I for the first time found myself with the "power". My father who was stronger than superman to me and my abuser who was the most powerful person that I feared was now weaker than most. I was conflicted as I helped him eat or button his shirt, the urge to get back at him was there. I remember one day when I came to visit him at the rehab apartment he had on a tee shirt and his under wear. I wanted so much to yell at him to put on his clothes and to walk out the door and never come back. For a moment I felt like the weak child that was on that couch the first time he ever molested me. I fought through these feelings after I reflected on how he couldn't even control his balance well. I decided to put the abuse out of my mind and do what I thought was right and be there for him.

Fr. V. would recover some and would be placed as Chaplain of Mercy Nursing Center in the south suburbs of Chicago. He would have ongoing continued problems from his condition while placed at Mercy. He would never be the great man or the evil molester he was. On June 9, 1994 the day before he died he was rushed to the emergency room at Rush Presbyterian St. Luke Hospital. He had them call me. I rushed over and was shocked to see him in such a weakened condition. I cried. When his sister Darlene whom I had never had a cross word with saw me she began yelling at me to leave and that I wasn't his family. I couldn't believe it. Fr. V. told the doctor I was his son and to let me come back to see him. He told me to leave and that he would be ok. He told me not to listen to Darlene. He said he loved me and I hugged him and left. He would die after emergency surgery. His funeral was at Holy Angels Catholic Church in Chicago. Cardinal

Bernardin officiated and a host of other priest assisted. I remember as I walked past the casket and gave hugs to the family which was my family since 12 years old, Darlene said "Kenneth why are you over there come sit next to me you are supposed to be here, you are family. I gave her a hug and went back to my seat in the back. What was interesting is how people came to me and gave me condolences even though I was not in the front row. A lot of the guys were there to say goodbye to Fr. V. It will still take ten years for the true story of what Fr. V. did to the boys in the parishes he served to come out. The stories are still coming out. When the story is finished I believe Fr. Victor Edward Stewart will go down in history as the priest who abused more boys than any other. I have forgiven Fr. Stewart. His judgment however is between him and God. I am committed to working in a proactive manner to eliminate the free roam that Fr. Stewart had in society. No more secrets and no more turning away at the signs. Datelines' NBC's to" Catch a Predator" and Oprah Winfrey's exposure about the horrors of pedophilia are to be commended. But it will take more than them on the battle line, it will take all who want children protected from sexual predators…………even if they are a priest.

In finally relating my full story publicly, I'm certain that it will raise a number of questions in many people's minds. That's OK, and something that I fully expect. After all, the general public has been exposed to the clergy abuse scandal for several years now, yet for many the subject remains not only taboo, but one that is shrouded in mystery. That's because, unless you were unfortunate enough to have it affect your life directly, most people have only read snippets here and there in the newspapers or heard quick sound bites on TV. So they don't understand all of the details of how things truly unfolded. When they discuss the topic, they therefore are usually going to have more questions than answers.

In this section I would like to share with you my observations as one who has seen the scandal from the inside. As you will see, some of the preconceived ideas you might have had may be off the mark. When dealing with a subject that so many have deliberately distorted, of course there is going to be lots of confusion. Hopefully, I can help to bring all of this into sharper focus for you, so that as you mull over these important topics you will be armed with the truth.

One of the most common questions people have in a case like mine is, why didn't I report my abuser? Why didn't I just leave him? Why did I let him get away with it for so long?

All excellent questions, though none of them have easy answers. The only way to really understand the situation is to put yourself in my shoes, trying to imagine what it must have been like to be a 12 year old boy who was confused and too scared to tell anybody what was happening to me. The kind of abuse that I suffered wasn't some sort of one time traumatic incident, which would be bad enough. No, this was a deliberate and carefully carried out seduction that this educated grown man used to manipulate the thoughts and feelings of a vulnerable and naïve adolescent child.

Looking back on it now I realize that his every move was fiendishly calculated. He was a man who made himself an expert at exploiting his position and the prestige and authority that it afforded him. All of the adults respected him, and the kids all liked him and wanted to be around him. When it came to children, he knew how to spread around money to—eventually—get what he wanted. He would buy a kid games, clothes, take him out to eat at restaurants. The whole nine yards. Especially when it came to a kid from a background where he hasn't had too many material things in his life, it's easy to imagine how appealing his free-spending overtures and acts of "kindness" would be. Of course, it was all a charade covering up his real intentions, as I discovered all too soon.

Still, though, I know people wonder why, as soon as he crossed the line and molested me, why didn't I go home right away and tell my mother? On the surface, that may sound like it should have been an easy and viable option for me. However, in reality it was a far different story. You see, my mother, like just about everybody else, was taken in by this man. He gained her trust. She thought he was doing a wonderful favor for her, taking care of me and therefore taking me off of her hands. I knew that she was very grateful for what she perceived as help, and I couldn't imagine what she would think if I walked up to her one day and told her about the disgusting things he was doing to me. I figured that she would never believe me. She would think I was making up stories and leveling false accusations to cover up something that I had actually done wrong. Poor Fr. V., would be seen as the innocent victim of an ungrateful child's smear campaign. Telling her, I became convinced, would take the bad situation I was in and make it even worse.

As time went on, however, I also came to believe that my mother *did* know what was going on, but she was in denial about it. Or, to give her the benefit of the doubt, even if she somehow didn't know what was going on, it was again a case of denial—she didn't *want to know* exactly what was going on. Oftentimes it is much easier for people to simply close their eyes rather than to confront an ugly truth.

Of course, there are many reasons why I, like so many others, did not come forward earlier, while the abuse was still taking place. Consider for a moment the intense feelings of shame and embarrassment that assail a young boy who is being subjected to sexual abuse. Adolescence is a confusing enough time for all kids. Now add into the mix an unhealthy sexual involvement with an older man, someone whom I was supposed to trust. Talk about conflicted and confusing emotions! Although I was attracted to girls, it was impossible to not worry that others would question my own sexual orientation. I worried that other kids would find out. Imagine what the boys would think of me. Not to mention the girls. I was horrified to think that they might consider me to be gay. At times, I would even question myself about the subject, despite the fact that in my own mind I felt heterosexual and I'd had relationships with girls. The bottom line: going public would mean an avalanche of emotional and psychological turmoil for me, and it was something I was just not capable of dealing with at the time.

Finally, as much as I disliked what Fr. V. was doing to me, at the same time I pretty much considered him to be my parent. So to reveal our secret would mean losing a parent, someone who, despite it all, did in fact take care of me. Furthermore, this very manipulative man used his cunning to make me feel like I meant the world to him. He spoiled me, buying me all of the material things that I wanted. I was being controlled and manipulated, yes, but not by some stranger. It was by a man I had for all intents and purposes come to think of as my father.

How then, did I eventually come to the point of going public about the abuse? When I became a young man, I made two attempts to speak up. But, as it turned out, I resolved that the best thing that I could do was to put it all behind me and just move on with my life. Which I did.

Over the course of time, however, I came to realize that this was not something that I could keep silent about. I reached a point where, because of the career, position and status I had attained, I could come forward and my claims would be seen as legitimate. My brother, who had also been abused by this same man, was the one who first approached me about speaking out. He had already begun the process of going public with his story, and telling my story, I realized, would lend even more credibility to his. So I finally agreed to unveil all of the secrets, and once I was fully committed to the process, I was determined that there would be no turning back. I would go wherever the story took me. I spoke out for myself, but even more importantly I felt that I was speaking out on behalf of others who had been victimized. They had been without a voice for far too long.

This brings us to the other great question that people always want to know about. What has going through the trauma of clergy sexual abuse done to my faith as a Catholic? How do I feel about the Church today, and what are my opinions about the clergy abuse scandal and how it was handled? Excellent questions…and again no easy answers. However, I can certainly say this much, I have seen the scandal—this dirty little secret—from the inside. I was a boy who grew up in the rectory from the age of 13 until young adulthood. For the vast majority of that time I was being abused by a priest, a man who had gained my trust and respect, only to use it for his own selfish purposes.

That was bad enough. Yet, like adding salt to a wound, this dreadful situation was made even worse by the insidious fact that "everyone" knew what was going on. This includes people such as the other priest who saw what Fr. V. was doing to me that day when he first touched me in a sexual way. This man could have intervened.

But he chose to do nothing. And it wasn't just him. Others knew certain things, too, and chose to look the other way. For example, the Archdiocese knew that I was living at the rectory, but nobody seemed to suspect anything.

Only later, when the clergy sexual abuse scandal broke nationwide, did I and everybody else come to learn the full extent of it. How the Church would find out about an abusive priest and, rather than turn him over to the law and / or defrock him, they would simply give him some counseling, move him to another parish a few miles away, and pretend as if that made the problem go away. Now, anyone who knows even the slightest thing about pedophiles (or cares even a tiny bit about the safety and welfare of children) can see that this is a ludicrous "solution" to a serious and pervasive problem. Officials within the Church chose the "ostrich with its head in the sand" approach instead of doing the right thing in the first place. Why? In my opinion, mostly to avoid the embarrassment and outrage that the truth surely would have unleashed. So, for decades, they managed to keep it all nicely bottled up.

Once the cork finally popped open, of course, it was a disaster for the Church. Forget the financial cost. That was nothing compared to the damage that it did to the trust and faith of countless people who were shocked and outraged that something like this could happen in their beloved Church. It was very sad indeed.

In my opinion, there is still a gigantic amount of work to be done on the part of the Church to even begin making amends for this scandal and all who have been hurt by it. The leadership needs to somehow find a way to win back the trust of the average man or woman in the pew. A good place to start would be to humbly acknowledge all that went wrong, without any excuses. To some degree this has already begun. But we are only at the beginning of a very long road. It took many years for things to get this bad. It would be naïve to imagine they will somehow get better overnight.

As for me, my relationship with my Church has forever been fractured. Yet my faith in God has not been shaken. No, not at all. Rather, it is those who are supposed to represent Him whom I will no longer blindly trust. They are, after all, sinners, capable, like the rest of us, of all kinds of bad things. Some of these bad things, of course, happened to me directly. But even if they had not, knowing now of all the crimes committed against other children, I think I would still come to these same conclusions. That priests are frail human beings, no different in their core nature than the average parishioner, and therefore we should never go on the assumption that they are somehow "above" sin. That is true only of Jesus Christ. Not of priests, or the Church itself (in the sense that those who lead the Church are human beings subject to sin). For these exceedingly sobering reasons, I now view my Church through very different lenses.

For the past 17 years as an adult, I have struggled with my involvement with the Church. I still consider myself Catholic, but for a long while my attendance at Church was filled with conflict. My wife converted to Catholicism before we married, but that was something that I wanted mostly for the stability of our family and the values we wanted to raise our future children with. Still, because of the troubled past I'd had with the Church I had no trust in the advice the priest gave during our pre-marital instruction. But I never lost my faith and trust in God.

Today, having gone public with my story, I feel that my past can actually help me to be more effective in my job in the field of Child Welfare. In fact, I don't consider it a job at all. It's much more than that. I know what it's like to be abused and to feel all alone. I have lived that pain, and I know how important it is to be an understanding listener. I try to live every day of my life with the passion of one who has dedicated himself to serving the vulnerable and making sure that never again do their cries go unheeded.

My life in many ways has now come full circle. My relationship with my Church is at peace now. I have learned the value of genuine forgiveness, and how it makes us more Christ-like to extend mercy when we have been wronged. I hold no grudges. By letting go of my anger and bitterness, it can no longer control me. There is a tremendous freedom in that.

I think I have found a parish I can call home now. The congregation feels like the community we had at St. Charles Lwanga before the arrival of Fr. V. and all that ensued. Instead, I feel the love and the faith of my brothers and sisters, which compels me to serve in genuine Christian charity. I am not unrealistic, though, and I know that I am not all the way back yet. But I am nonetheless looking forward to my son's first communion, confirmation, and all the other good and sacred aspects of our tradition. I think I may even become a deacon someday. It is my prayer that the Church of tomorrow can learn from the grievous mistakes and scandals of yesterday. This book is my testimony, my humble contribution toward that lofty goal.

From Abused to Protector

Kenneth F. Joe Sr.
"A Triumphant Survivor"

Kenneth has redefined the meaning of victim. By sharing his story he has taken away the cloud of shame and embarrassment associated with sexual abuse and has illuminated the characteristics of a true warrior, successfully reclaiming his life. Kenneth has taught us all how to live battle ready.

Denice Murray, MA
Associate Deputy Director
Illinois Department of Children and Family Services

Kenneth embraces the writing of this book with the same passion, intensity and care that he has demonstrated during his entire professional tenure...Without question, this book allows the victim to become victorious and reveals a new purpose for living and appreciating one's life...

Donald J. Dew, ACSW
President/CEO
Habilitative Systems, Inc.

Having had the pleasure of working for Kenneth in his quest for protecting our children, he has always shown exemplary courage, integrity, character and leadership. Kenneth motivates all those that come into his path and his influence and passion for children is contagious. His passion for being an advocate for justice for our children shows his determination to make a difference in their lives. He has allowed the power of forgiveness to transform his destiny into living a victorious life and leading others to live victorious, as well. He didn't allow his past to determine who he would become in the future. He moved from victim to victor! I pledge to support him in his fight to keep our children safe. This book is sure to be a blessing to all those who read it.

Keisha Smith-Poole
Consultant

www.ingramcontent.com/pod-product-compliance
Lightning Source LLC
Chambersburg PA
CBHW032058150426
43194CB00006B/573